Treasure in
Earthen Vessels

Treasure in Earthen Vessels

*Homilies about God's Good News in the
Lives of Real People Like You and Me*

JOSEPH MARK VOUGHT

RESOURCE *Publications* · Eugene, Oregon

TREASURE IN EARTHEN VESSELS
Homilies about God's Good News in the Lives of Real People Like You and Me

Resource Publications
An Imprint of Wipf and Stock Publishers
199 W. 8th Ave., Suite 3
Eugene, OR 97401

www.wipfandstock.com

PAPERBACK ISBN: 978-1-6667-3443-0
HARDCOVER ISBN: 978-1-6667-9027-6
EBOOK ISBN: 978-1-6667-9028-3

12/08/21

Contents

Introduction

"Since it is by God's mercy that we are engaged in this ministry, we do not lose heart . . . For we do not proclaim ourselves; we proclaim Jesus Christ as Lord and ourselves as your slaves for Jesus' sake . . . But we have this treasure in clay jars, so that it may be made clear that this extraordinary power belongs to God and does not come from us. We are afflicted in every way, but not crushed; perplexed, but not driven to despair; persecuted, but not forsaken; struck down, but not destroyed; always carrying in the body the death of Jesus, so that the life of Jesus may also be made visible in our bodies." (2 Cor 4:1–10)[1]

Paul of Tarsus was a most unlikely convert to the good news of Jesus Christ. Writing to the church at Corinth, circa 53 AD, some years after his confrontation on the Damascus Road and commissioning by the risen Christ, Paul explains, "For I am the least of the apostles, unfit to be called an apostle, because I persecuted the church of God. But by the grace of God, I am what I am, and his grace toward me has not been in vain." (1 Cor 15:9–10) Paul realized salvation was no longer a matter of being righteous before God but trusting God's love, the forgiveness of sins, and the promise of salvation. As Paul would say, "For by grace you have been saved through faith, and this is not your own doing; it is the gift of God." (Eph 2:8) This is the good news of Jesus that Paul, the apostles, and countless Christians have lived and proclaimed across the history

---

1. All Scripture citations are from the New Revised Standard Version Bible, Copyright 1989, Division of Christian Education of the National Council of Churches of Christ in the United States of America.

of the church. It is also the good news that is seen, heard, and lived in the daily lives of Christians shared with others. C.S. Lewis said, "People are mirrors, or 'carriers' of Christ to other people . . . This 'good infection' can be carried by those who have not got it themselves. Usually, it is those who know Him that bring Him to others. That is why the whole body of Christians showing Him to one another is so important."[2]

I am a Christian in no small part because of the love and nurture of parents who brought me as an infant to the church for Holy Baptism. Having been raised in a pastor's family, I resisted the idea of ever becoming a pastor myself. God has a sense of humor and after thirty-six years in ordained ministry in four parish settings, hospice ministry, prison ministry, and chaplaincy at the National Cathedral in Washington, DC, I am humbled and honored by the call. All along the way, family, friends, parishioners, unlikely saints, and many others have shared the treasure of Christ and the Gospel with me in their lives and witness. The following homilies and sermons feature a story or illustration from the lives of real people I've been privileged to know, or know of, all of them earthen vessels who have carried the treasure of the Gospel. Some names have been changed to protect the innocent. I am grateful for all of them.

Rev. Joseph M. Vought

2. *The Business of Heaven*, Daily Readings from C.S. Lewis, p. 306 Hooper, Walter ed Fount Paperbacks. 4th Impression, 1987.

"Hitler Youth turned Lutheran Pastor"

Easter Season/April 10, 2016/
Community Lutheran Church

JOHN 21:1–19; ACTS 9:1–20

EASTER WAS A DAY of surprise for the women who thought they knew what life and death was all about. Easter is rebirth and a new creation. It's about God who brings life out of death, joy from sadness, love where there was hatred, and works totally contrary to our human expectations and assumptions. But let's be honest, we are more at home with our own experiences or our own ideas of what we think is true. How often have we closed ourselves off to any idea that God could do a new thing? How often have we thought we knew better? Peter, who always thought he knew more than he really did, looked into the empty tomb on Easter day and then went home. Today in our Gospel he says to his fellow disciples, "I am going fishing," as if to say, "This Jesus whom we followed must have been a dream . . . too good to be true." Look what happens: Jesus, the risen Lord, meets Peter like he did on that first day by the lakeshore. He is caught again by Jesus who is cooking fish on a charcoal fire, just like the charcoal fire where Peter warmed himself in the courtyard of the high priest when he denied Jesus three times. Peter is confronted by Jesus and then forgiven. He experiences grace and is called again to preach forgiveness and the good news to others.

The other Easter story before us is the story of Paul. There is a before and after quality about his life. I mean he had a resume:

"If anyone has reason to be confident in the flesh, I have more: circumcised on the eighth day, a member of the people of Israel, of the tribe of Benjamin, a Hebrew born of Hebrews; as to the law, a Pharisee; as to zeal, a persecutor of the church; as to righteousness under the law, blameless. Yet whatever gains I had I have come to regard as loss because of Christ." (Phil 3:4–7) I don't know which is more amazing: that God chose a man like Paul to become the greatest of all apostles, or that God moved a disciple named Ananias to put aside his fear and welcome a murderer. For Ananias to learn about Saul and be asked to welcome him would be like Pope Francis receiving El Chapo Guzman. Jesus confronts zealous Saul, knocks him down, and speaks, "I am Jesus whom you are persecuting." (Acts 9:5) Like Peter, Paul must be confronted with his lack of faith, struck blind, and then be led and fed, like a baby to have hands laid-on, be baptized by Ananias, and raised up to be God's new creation. The term conversion doesn't do it justice. For Paul, like Peter, it must have been like dying and rising, but that's how Easter happens when faith overcomes fear and God brings life out of death. God does it; we don't.

My own life and vocation were influenced by a European pastor named Eric Gritsch, born in Austria and raised as Hitler came to power. His father, a Lutheran pastor, worked for the resistance against Hitler and when discovered, was sent to a labor camp and died there. Eric was then pressed into the Hitler Youth and became a leader of a Werewolf pack of boys who did guerilla warfare. Toward the end of the war, Eric learned they were facing sixteen thousand Russian soldiers on the Eastern Front. He gave the order to desert and told his boys, "I will no longer give my life to the insanity of a man named Hitler." He buried his Nazi uniform, stole farm clothes, and walked into the Russian lines, passing himself off as a refugee. After the war, Eric went to Vienna where he studied with Victor Frankl, a Jew who survived the Holocaust. Like Ananias and Paul, the Jewish survivor and former Nazi told their stories to each other. Frankl said to Gritsch, "You should become a Lutheran pastor." Eric became a Lutheran pastor, then a theologian and one of the world's leading Luther scholars. He taught my dad, he taught me, and I am grateful for his Godly life and witness.[1]

When strangers are brought closer by the love of God, where judgment gives way to justice and fear opens a way for faith, Easter happens. The good news of Jesus frees us from ourselves and all the other gods that would enslave us. Because of the forgiveness of sins and grace given to us by so many others, we live by faith, we trust God's amazing grace, and we are God's Easter people. We can say with St. Paul, "We see in a mirror dimly, then we shall see God face to face . . . " (1 Cor 13:12) "Oh the depth and the riches and the wisdom of God! How unsearchable are His judgments and inscrutable His ways?" (Romans 11:33) And finally, "I have been crucified with Christ; therefore, it is no longer I who live but Christ who lives in me." (Gal 2:20)

Let us pray: Living Lord of Easter, convict us when we are headstrong and stuck in our ways. Help us to experience the surprise and joy of being wrong. Surround us with people who will forgive us and love us as we grow. Help us to die to ourselves that we may live for you. Make us channels and instruments of your peace and messengers of your good news for the world you love and came to save. Amen.

---

1. *The Boy From the Burgenland: From Hitler Youth to Seminary Professor*, Copyright 2006 by Eric W. Gritsch. Infinity Publishing Company, 2007. Interview with Eric W. Gritsch, April 10, 2012.

"Fallible People, Faithful God"

Advent Season/December 19, 2010/
Community Lutheran Church

MATTHEW 1:18–25

I WILL NEVER FORGET the births of our children, Kristin and Jonathan. I will tell you that labor and delivery for both of our children was arduous and miraculous. Because I received my wife's permission, I can tell you that each of our children took nearly twenty-four hours of labor to arrive. I was nearly wiped out from it all, to say nothing of Debra who did all the work. At one point during Kristin's birth, I said, "If I don't get something to eat, I am going to faint and will not be here for the birth of our child." Debra, who was in no mood for my weakness, said, "Joseph, if you're not back here, I will have the doctor operate on you!" I made a quick dash to the cafeteria but I was in the room when Kristin arrived. I was there for the birth of our son Jonathan too. Looking back on it all now, my personal theory is that Lamaze breathing is merely something to keep the father occupied while the mother, the baby, and God do all the work. I think I was a good husband and labor coach, but I knew from the "get-go" that it was out of my hands. Something of God was at work, a new world was beginning, and I was simply blessed and amazed to be there at all.

On this fourth Sunday of Advent, can you imagine Joseph? He almost didn't make it for the birth of Jesus! In Luke we have the story of Jesus' birth from Mary's point of view. Today we hear

Joseph's side of the story. If Mary was amazed by the angel's news of her pregnancy, can you imagine Joseph? Matthew tells us, "When Mary had been engaged to Joseph but before they came together, she was found to be with child from the Holy Spirit." (Matthew 1:18) Joseph heard the news before the angel came to him and as he considered the matter, he knew there could be no good end to the story. He knew he had not been with Mary, so what was he to think? No matter what he might say, people would suspect him. The tongues would wag in the village, "Hey, he couldn't wait for the wedding night," and Mary, Joseph and their families would be disgraced. And that wasn't the worst. Deuteronomy stipulated that if a woman was found to be with child before the wedding night she could be brought up on charges and stoned to death for adultery. Joseph could have exposed her. Can you imagine his confusion and bewilderment? Sometimes problems in life are such that there are simply no good options and no good endings. If I expose her, I save my honor and she could be killed, but I couldn't live with that. If I dismiss her and walk away, I abandon her and shame myself. So, ". . . Joseph, being a righteous man and unwilling to expose her to public disgrace, planned to dismiss her quietly." (Matthew 1:19) No good decision; just the lesser of two bad options.

When Joseph finally falls into a fitful sleep and is visited by the angel, we would like to believe that somehow all of his problems were laid to rest, but hearing the angel say, "Do not be afraid to take Mary as your wife, for the child conceived in her is from the Holy Spirit" (Matthew 1:20) does not take away the predicament or the problem. The problems of pregnant Mary, a bewildered Joseph, and a scandalous birth remain and walk side by side with God's amazing news, "The child conceived in her is from the Holy Spirit. She will bear a son, and you are to name him Jesus, for he will save his people from their sins." (Matthew 1:20–21)

But isn't this the way God always works? The promises of God are always trying to be born among real human people of flesh and blood. Joseph is called to be a person of faith when fear is all around. Where there is conflict, confusion, and no easy answer, there is also a call to courage and commitment when it would be easier to cut and run.

In the midst of an impossible situation, Mary, in Luke's Gospel, said to the angel, "Behold I am the servant of the Lord; let it be to me according to your Word." (Luke 1:38) And Joseph, while he never speaks a word in today's Gospel, got up and did as the angel of the Lord commanded him. Martin Luther reminded us that faith always trusts the promises of God even in the midst of the most desperate and unlikely situations.[1] When we think there is no good ending, God is the one who brings a new creation and makes all things new. But then that's always how God has worked. When we think things are impossible, are tempted to run away or react with disbelief, we must hear the angels say, "nothing will be impossible with God." (Luke 1:37) Because they listened and obeyed, Joseph and Mary were there for the birth of Jesus and played their part in the promises of God. Christmas and the promises of God are always trying to be born among us. God invites us to believe, obey, and walk by faith. Amen.

---

1. "In ourselves, we are sinners, and yet through faith we are righteous by the imputation of God. For we trust him who promises to deliver us, and in the meantime struggle so that sin may not overwhelm us, but that we may stand up to it until he finally takes it away from us." Luther's Works, Volume 25 (Lectures on Roman Glosses and Scholia) (ed. Concordia Pub House, 1972)

"Baptized and Blessed"

The Baptism of Our Lord/January 9, 2005/
Muhlenberg Lutheran Church

MATTHEW 3:13–17

IN TWO SHORT WEEKS, we have come thirty years from Jesus' birth to the Baptism of Our Lord. In Advent, we recalled his questionable birth and the angel's visit to Mary, a young girl pregnant before her time and Joseph's struggle whether to divorce her. At Christmas, we saw Jesus in the manger. But there is not much more about Jesus' childhood. Remember the Holy Family fleeing to Egypt because of King Herod's murderous rage? Then, after King Herod's death, how they returned to Nazareth? The only other story is of Jesus getting lost at the age of twelve when the family made a trip to Jerusalem. His parents came upon him in the temple with the teachers, listening and asking them questions. When they questioned Jesus, he replied, "Did you not know I must be in my father's house?" (Luke 2:49)

Jesus grows up quickly in the Gospels. The next time we see him is as a young man, standing on the banks of the Jordan for baptism. John the Baptist protests that he is the one who should be baptized by Jesus. Jesus says, "Let it be so now; for it is proper for us in this way to fulfill all righteousness." (Matthew 3:15) It is a strange answer. Jesus is saying to John, "You may not understand it, it may seem totally backwards, but this Baptism is part of God's plan." For Jesus, his baptism is as important as his birth. Baptism, like the event of our birth, always tells us something about our identity, who we are, and from where we come.

When Jesus steps into the water, he joins himself to our humanity. He is once more the Word become Flesh, Emmanuel, our God who is so totally with us that he dives all the way in. If there is any doubt, we learn in the voice from heaven, who it is who wades into the water and takes on our life, "This is my Son, the Beloved . . . " (Matthew 3:17) For all we know about Jesus' birth, his anxious faithful parents, his strange childhood, the hidden years between the age of twelve, and the time of his Baptism, what we see in this Baptism is God's anointing and rejoicing in Jesus.

So, it is with us . . . in baptism, we learn something about our identity. Before my baptism, I was born on January 3rd 1957 to John and Joyce Vought. While my birth was cause for rejoicing, there was also great anxiety. I was born two months premature, in a day and time when premature babies were high risk and did not often survive. I weighed a whopping three pounds, seven ounces and for the first two months of my life, I lived in an incubator at the hospital. Not only was my birth difficult, but my conception took place during my parents' engagement before they were married. Times being what they were, both families were not very understanding or helpful and, in fact, they made my parents feel ashamed and terrible. The great white wedding was cancelled and they were quickly hustled off to a side altar to be married by the local pastor. Until I learned the story of my parent's wedding and the events surrounding my birth, I always wondered why they never celebrated their anniversary. So, when I was baptized on September 29th, 1957 at Christ Lutheran Church in Mifflinburg, Pennsylvania, the pastor spoke the word and the water flowed, "I baptize you Joseph Mark Vought in the name of the Father, and of the Son, and of the Holy Spirit. You are a child of God." My mom and dad told me it was one of the first times they could celebrate, one of the first moments in their young married life when there was no cause for shame and no guilt. There was forgiveness and a promise of grace and new life.

Baptism is about our identity. In the liturgy for Holy Baptism, we say, "We are born children of a fallen humanity; by water and the Holy Spirit we are reborn children of God and made members of the church, the body of Christ."[1] My mom and dad gave me the gift of life, but they did something more profound than that, they had me baptized. They, and the family of God into which I was baptized, celebrated me and taught me from the moment of my baptism, whatever else I was, whatever the circumstances of my birth and background, whatever else I became or did not become, I would always be first and foremost a child of God. I am a Christian and a pastor in no small part because of the love and grace and the faith they passed on to me in my baptism.

Wherever you come from, whatever pain or heartache you bear in your life, no matter what lies in your past or in the future's path, you will always have God's promise over your life. As an infant, a teenager, or an adult, baptism joins us to the story and the community of Jesus. His life is our life, His path is our path and while your Baptism is personal, it is never private. From the moment of your baptism, you are not only blessed by God, the Father, joined to Jesus, and anointed by the Spirit, you are brought into a family of God and joined to the Body of Christ. Someone has said, "Baptismal water is always thicker than blood." We honor the family but we do not worship the family. Life will change, families grow up, loved ones will move away or die, life will turnover, and what you think is stability and permanence will change before your very eyes. But in the Body of Christ, where two or three are gathered in Jesus' name around the Word of God, a water-filled font, a table of grace, and forgiveness with bread and wine, we are called again to remember who we are and whose we are. Your baptism is not a family celebration but a celebration of the family of God. That is why we literally take the babies out of the arms of the parents and walk the newly baptized one into the congregation. My parents baptized me, but they are not my primary family.

This is why we take baptism seriously. This is why we live it together because we live in a culture that tries to tell us in a thousand different ways who we are and who we ought to be. So, we must affirm our baptism again and again. And for all those who have fallen away or become inactive, for all those baptized ones who can't quite

1. "Evangelical Lutheran Worship," Holy Baptism, p. 227. Copyright 2006 Evangelical Lutheran Church in America, Augsburg Fortress Publishers.

believe it, we must reach out to them and tell them. This is why we commune and sing together and help each other to remember that we are God's beloved and baptized children. With God's promise over our lives, with an identity like that, and this body of Christ, we can do good work, love our families, build this church, and serve this community. We can walk as children of the light and follow Jesus wherever he wants us to go. All because of our baptisms, in the name of the Father and of the Son, and of the Holy Spirit.

"In the water and the witness, in the breaking of the bread, in the waiting arms of Jesus who is risen from the dead. God has made a new beginning from the ashes of our past, in the losing and the winning, we hold fast."[2] (Hymn #698 "With One Voice" Hymnal) Amen.

2. John Ylvisaker, "We Were Baptized in Christ Jesus," © 1985. Stanza 2 used by permission. Hymn 698, *With One Voice*, A Lutheran Resource for Worship, Augsburg Fortress, Minneapolis, 1995.

"Lord, We Are Not Worthy, only say the Word"

Season of Pentecost/June 2, 2013/
Community Lutheran Church

LUKE 7:1–10

HER NAME WAS ROSA, she was a devout Roman Catholic and she looked at me through the isolation tent in Intensive Care. "Chaplain, will you please bring me Holy Communion?" Rosa's husband was on an aircraft carrier in the Indian Ocean and she was in the ICU with an infection that required her to be in isolation. I told Rosa I would arrange for it, we prayed, I took off my mask and gown, and left the unit. I was serving as a chaplain at Bethesda Naval Medical Center, Washington, DC, the summer of 1981, after my second year of seminary. I was the duty-chaplain for the day and it was my responsibility to cover the ICU, the ER, and respond to any pastoral needs, but I was conflicted. I was not ordained. I was a seminarian and could not yet preside and give Holy Communion. I called the Captain, Director of Pastoral Care, a Baptist minister, and explained the request from Rosa and my dilemma. The captain listened patiently to my story and responded: "Chaplain, you've got the duty today and a patient has requested the sacrament. I don't care if you are ordained or not, following the Lutheran rules or not. She is looking to you as her pastor. You will commune her and give her the sacrament today, do you understand?" I responded, "Yes sir. I am reading you loud and clear." I am not in the military but I know a direct order when I hear one. So, with fear and trembling,

I took a communion kit, read through the liturgy aloud, practiced and worked on the posture, took a stole from the chaplain's closet, and communed Rosa that afternoon.

From a strict Lutheran standpoint, I had violated our church's practices and presided at Holy Communion as an un-ordained lay-person. We were from two different worlds. She was Roman Catholic and I was Lutheran. She was in isolation, away from her loved ones, in the hospital and afraid. I was wearing a mask and a gown, a clerical collar, and a stole, trying my best to imitate a Catholic priest, feeling way out of bounds, with no authority whatsoever. But I tell you, I will never forget presiding at my first communion with Rosa. If she sensed my nervousness, she never let on. When she received the host from me, she took it in her trembling hands as the very Body of Christ, with tears streaming down her face said, "Gracias a Dios! Thank you, Jesus!"

Jesus and the Centurion were from different worlds. The Centurion was a pagan who commanded 100 men in the Roman occupation force that controlled Galilee, Judea, and the Jews. Jesus was a charismatic Jewish rabbi who preached the Kingdom of God and was gaining attention for his miracles and healings in Galilee. Romans were pagans who believed the emperor in Rome was divine, yet this centurion was attracted to God's people and helped them build a synagogue. While he knew how to use power and influence, he also knew the limits of his power and asked Jesus to heal his servant who was suffering. The amazing thing is that Jesus and the Centurion never meet. While Jesus was on his way, the Centurion realized his limits, confessed his unworthiness, and made a great confession, "Lord I am not worthy to receive you but only say the Word and my servant shall be healed." (Luke 7:6-7) Luke reports, "When Jesus heard this, he was amazed, 'I tell you not even in Israel have I found such faith.'" (Luke 7:9)

Rosa knew that she needed Jesus and thank God the Captain, Director of Pastoral Care, straightened me out when I was afraid, nervous, and thought it was all about me. The grace of God and the love of Jesus has nothing to do with our authority and power. We can only bow and bend before God's amazing grace, but we can invite others to meet Jesus and become witnesses and carriers of God's grace. That's why we say it is the Lord's Supper, not the Lutheran supper. It is faith that trusts God's Word that comes in the forgiveness of sins, the passing of God's peace, and Jesus' presence in bread and wine. It is God's grace that brings unlikely people together, to heal and be a new creation. It was grace and trust in God's Word that brought a Roman Centurion into the compass and compassion of a loving Savior. Just as it was the Word of the Lord and the real presence of Jesus that brought Rosa and me together in Holy Communion, from different worlds, when we were both afraid.

We live in a world where we use power and influence to make a difference in our lives. But you and I know that life and power have limits. It is good to remember that life is a gift and grace is from God and it's not always about us and what we do. Then it is the highest wisdom to say, "Lord, I am not worthy to receive you but only say the Word and I shall be healed." (Luke 7:6–7) Amen.

"Trucker in a Birdbath"

Easter Season/May 6, 2012/Community Lutheran

ACTS 8:26–40

IN THE SUMMER OF 2001, I had just finished a Bible study in the garden outside my former church in Harrisonburg. I was chatting with a member when a big eighteen-wheeler came down the hill on Market Street, down-shifted with a roar, and rumbled into our parking lot. Noisy air brakes brought the rig to a stop, the door opened and slammed, and around the front of the cab stepped a mountain of a man. He was wearing black jeans, a big belt, and silver buckle that I could barely see beneath his barrel chest. It was covered by a T-shirt with a large number three and on his head, a cap with Dale Earnhart's signature. He walked like he meant business. His arms were bigger than my thighs. "One of y'all a preacher?" The church member looked at him and said, "Sure, he is," pointing to me and then half-ran-walked to his car and drove off.

"Name's Jimmy Williams, from Georgia, heading' home to see my family but I need to talk to you about getting baptized. I been on the road to Baltimore and back, just come off I-81, and said to myself, "Okay Lord, it'll be the first church I see, and you're the one." "Jimmy, I said, "how about you tell me a little about yourself." Jimmy's story was like a sad country song: a busted first marriage, followed by hard driving, hard-drinking and, hard-living, then marriage to an old girlfriend and the birth of a baby, forming a family who stood by him before Alcoholics Anonymous began to take hold. "She's a good church-goin' woman and I should go with her but I ain't never been baptized or gone to church and well, we had a fight about it before I left and I been thinking' and praying' for the better part of two hundred miles. I'm still one heckuva mess to live with some days and Lord knows I can be stubborn but I'm ready now cuz you know God give her to me and that little boy too and well that's why I'm here: to thank God and get right. Can you baptize me?" I responded, "Don't you think you'd like to get baptized at home so your family can celebrate it?" Jimmy said, "Nope, wife said if I was ready, just do it. Whenever I try going my own way, I usually get messed up, so I am here for Jesus and baptism and to get going the right way." "Okay, let's go in the church." "No preacher, could we do it here? That bird-bath there will do just fine." So, after a promise from Jimmy that he would go to church next Sunday and worship as often as he could, Jimmy knelt in the grass and I baptized that trucker in the birdbath. When the eighteen-wheeler rolled out of the parking lot, Jimmy was waving and smiling, blowing his horn all the way to Route 81.

In this Easter season, we have seen the risen Christ bringing peace to his disciples, gathering them like a good shepherd, and calling them to invite others. When we abide in the vine, Christ says, we can't help but bear fruit and be a blessing to others. When you see it, it is good to celebrate. I am proud of our youth who made over a hundred thousand meals with other Christians for hungry people in Asia and Africa. I am proud of those who served "Christmas in April" to repair the home of a needy family in our community. And I am proud of our Lutheran Synod, trying to be Christ's hands for a needy world fighting malaria in Africa and speaking a word of hope. When you are led by the Spirit, you never know where it will take you or whom you will meet. It is the story of the church in Acts where Jesus sends out followers to tell the good news in Jerusalem, Samaria, and the ends of the earth.

Today, Philip, a deacon in the early church, is sent into the wilderness where he meets an Ethiopian eunuch. We learn that this man was drawn to the faith of Israel, returning from worship in Jerusalem when Philip met him on the road. He was a court official and he could read. But he was also suspect because he was a foreigner and worst of all, he was a eunuch which means he was probably forcibly sterilized so he could serve the Queen without being a threat to the King. Jewish law said he was damaged goods, could not produce children, and was unable to participate fully in worship, but perfect love casts out fear and Philip goes to his chariot. When the eunuch reads about the lamb led to the slaughter who, like himself, was cutoff and humiliated, he wonders who else has been so humiliated. This is what happens when we open up Scripture in the company of others. It touches our life and reveals the risen Christ. Philip proclaims Jesus, the Lamb who was slain, risen as a Good Shepherd to embrace all people, including this African brother. Now it is Easter all over again, streams bursting forth in the desert and by the road as the eunuch asks, "What is to prevent me from being baptized?" As they opened Scripture together, now they go down into the water together, where a child of Africa is raised up a new child of God. By the end of it all, Philip is caught up by the Spirit and the eunuch goes on his way rejoicing, blessed to be a blessing.

When you are living the new life of Easter and led by the Spirit, you never know where it will take you or whom you will meet. I learned it all over again when I met Jimmy Williams from Georgia on the road by my church, where there was water in a bird bath, a forgiven sinner who was embraced by Jesus, was baptized and went on his way rejoicing. What roads will you travel this week and who will you meet?

The new life of the Risen Christ that made us new sons and daughters is the hope of the world. It's the best news there is because it reminds us that nothing is impossible with God, no one is ever cut off from God's love. When we believe and bear fruit, there is just no telling where the Spirit of God will lead us or who we will meet as a brother or sister. You don't have to be a preacher or a Philip, but you are baptized to be a servant of God and make a positive difference in the lives of others. A quote attributed to St. Francis is, "Preach Christ and proclaim Good News all the time, when you need to, use words." In whatever roads and pathways you travel this week, remember you are God's beloved. Try to look at everyone with the love of Jesus and may you be blessed to be the blessing. Amen.

"Jesus in a Ferrari"

Maundy Thursday/April 17, 2014/ Community Lutheran Church

EXODUS 12:1–4, 11–14; 1 CORINTHIANS 11:23–26; JOHN 13:1–17, 31B–35

DADDY, TELL ME A story, sing me a song.

This is the song I sang as a lullaby to my infant daughter, "Jesus loves me this I know for the Bible tells me so, little ones to him belong, they are weak but He is strong."[1] What were the songs you sang to your children? This is how we are raised and this is what we do as parents. A wise person said, "That all our lives are formed and shaped by songs and stories." We all have our favorite stories and songs. I know a parishioner who loves *Les Miserables* and I think she has probably watched it twenty times or more.

From one generation to another, this is what we do: we tell stories, we sing songs. This is what we do as people of faith. That is what worship is: we tell stories, we sing the stories in our songs, we gather around tables where even our meals proclaim a story. We act out the drama and great themes of our faith . . . of a call and a journey, danger and deliverance, exile and homecoming, betrayal and forgiveness, captivity and freedom, death and new life. We proclaim the faith of our ancestors, the hope of the prophets, we pray our

---

1. "Jesus Loves Me" written by Anna and Susan Warner, 1860; tune by William Bradbury, 1862 CC-BY-SA license.

faith and struggles today, and we look forward to the promise of life with all the saints in the new Jerusalem, the city of God.

Two nights ago, when our Jewish brothers and sisters gathered for Passover, the story began with the youngest child asking, "Why is this night different from all other nights?" Tell me the story again, help me to learn it so that I may tell it too. And so, the story goes. It's our story too. "Take a lamb for each family, a lamb for each household . . . divided in proportion to the number of people who eat of it so that all may eat of it. . . eat it, your loins girded, sandals on your feet, your staff in your hand; and you shall eat it hurriedly. It is the Passover of the Lord. . . a day of deliverance and remembrance for you . . ." (Exodus 12:3–11, 14)

On Palm Sunday, we made a procession with palms remembering and acting out Jesus' triumphal entry into Jerusalem. And then with Scripture as the script, we told the story of Jesus' Passion where we played the parts: one of your pastors was Jesus at the 8:15 worship service and one of our youths was Jesus at 11:00. Others played parts and we all played the people of Jerusalem, putting Jesus on trial, consenting to his death, crying, "Crucify him," then beholding his courage, carrying his cross, and loving us all the way to his dying breath.

It reminded me of a trip we took in 1990 to the Oberammergau Passion Play in Germany. The Passion Play is a dramatic retelling of our Lord's Passion in scripture, music, and song, lasting 4 hours long with an intermission for lunch. During our lunch break, someone in our tour group cried out, "Look there goes Jesus in a Ferrari!" The cast and crew were off to lunch too. The people of Oberammergau have been performing the Passion Play since 1634. It got me thinking, what would it be like if we did more of this with our youth, adults, and children, to not only read scripture, but memorize it and act it out? We might just learn it for God's sake.

Tonight, Maundy Thursday, then Good Friday and Holy Saturday. the story of God's deliverance is remembered, reenacted, and sung. This is the night of salvation. Scripture becomes the script. St. Paul says, "For I received from the Lord what I also handed on to you, that the Lord Jesus on the night He was betrayed took a loaf of bread and when he had given thanks, he broke it and said, 'This is my body, that is for you." (1 Cor11:23–24) One of your pastors dares to play Jesus. From John's Gospel, "Jesus knew his hour had come to depart from this world and go to the Father. Having loved his own who were in the world, he loved them to the end. . .And during supper Jesus got up from the table, tied a towel around himself and began to wash the disciple's feet. When he finished, he said, 'I have set you an example, you should do as I have done. . . I give you a new commandment, love one another as I have loved you." (John 13:1–15, 34) We come here to hear it and to reenact it in our worship.

As we live out these Three Sacred Days, we live the liturgy, we act out our faith, Scripture becomes the script, and even our hymns and songs tell the story. Wherever we go in this wide and wonderful world that God gives us, we worship, we tell the story of our faith, and of Jesus who loves us to the end. Like children who love to hear stories and sing songs over and over again, we hear the story again, we act it out, we sing our faith so that it may find a home within our hearts. We do it all with the hope that we may come to live and serve and give our lives away like Jesus.

"Jesu, Jesu, fill us with your love, show us how to serve, the neighbors we have from you."[2]

---

2. "Jesu, Jesu, Fill Us with Your Love" *Hymn # 765* Tom Colvin, With One Voice, A Lutheran Resource for Worship, Augsburg Fortress, Minneapolis, 1995.

"Berated and Blessed"

Pentecost Season/August 22, 2010/
Community Lutheran Church

LUKE 13:10–17

I WILL NEVER FORGET Jamie, that overweight kid in the small Pennsylvania town where I grew up. He was pudgy and big for his age. He was an only child born of elderly parents who doted on him. A mama's boy we called him. He had disabilities which affected his ability to learn and a strange neurological tick which caused his head to move continually. Jamie and his family were members of my dad's congregation and we were in Sunday School together.

During the weekdays after school, Jamie stayed mostly at home, closely monitored by his parents, while my friends and I were usually busy riding bikes or playing football in someone's backyard. But every now and then Jamie would get away from his parent's overprotective gaze. "Hey look, it's 'Jamie, the mama's boy,' one of my friends would call out. I always felt bad about it but I wouldn't say anything to defend Jamie because I wanted to be cool. Sometimes, I would try to change the subject, saying "Come on you guys, let's play football," and then, in an attempt to be friendly, I would say, "Hey Jamie, do you wanna play?" Jamie would smile eagerly and nod his head to be included. Of course, you can imagine what happened. While we would slam into each other with joy, things invariably got ugly with Jamie. Somehow, we took a special delight piling on the fat kid and Jamie would often go home crying and with a bloody nose. However, the next Sunday, Jamie would be with his family in church. In Sunday School, we sat next to each other and Jamie loved every minute of it, being with the other kids even though they would often laugh at him behind his back. I remember my mother scolding me, "Jamie is a very sensitive and kind boy! You and your friends ought to be ashamed." She was right and I knew it. I was ashamed of the way we treated him.

What was it like where you grew up? Did you have labels for people who were different in your school or community? Did you call people nerds, brains, greasers, mama's boys, or maybe worse? Did you have a nickname you were proud of or ashamed of? Have you ever been ashamed of the way you treated someone because of their appearance or reputation?

I wonder who was the woman in the synagogue. Was she known by her name or perhaps labeled with another? Maybe she was called the "old hunchback" or the "crooked woman." She was a part of the community, perhaps married, perhaps raised a family, maybe a person of good works but she is known only as "the bent woman." Defined only by her infirmity, I wonder if she had friends? Did the townsfolk make fun of her, treat her with contempt or did they just ignore her? She is the one who is bent and stooped, bearing upon her shoulders an invisible yet heavy burden, the burden of being different, of not looking like everyone else. She is there for everyone who is so named. He's just a drunk, a dimwit, blind as a bat, a fatso. She's there for Jamie, the mama's boy."

But on that day Jesus saw her and from out of the crowd, right in the middle of the service, Our Lord called to her. Jesus heals this woman, touches her life, and perhaps for the first time in her life, she is able to stand up straight and she begins to praise God. Right in the middle of the sermon or when the plates are being passed, Jesus touches her and this woman begins to praise God. Her life is changed, her infirmity healed, but perhaps the most beautiful and touching thing is the way Jesus speaks to her. Jesus looks upon her with the eyes of God and gives her a new name. Our Lord reconceives her identity and calls her a "daughter of Abraham." For the first time in her life, perhaps this woman hears words of grace, new life. "Daughter of Abraham? Me? The very one in whom God blessed all the nations of the earth and gave the promises of the covenant? Abraham, the one blessed to be a blessing. You mean I am an heir to that heritage?" Yes, dear sister, child of God, you are much more than any label the world can give you. God calls you blessed.

Now do you begin to see what a wonderful sacrament of healing and grace the church can be? For people who have been victimized by the world's labeling, we are to look on them with God's eyes and see in them great and precious promises. This church is the place where we begin to look on each other and the world with new eyes, to see God in the most unlikely places and to help people reconceive of themselves so they might no longer be bound but free, and blessed to be a blessing.

Of course, the wonder of it all is that it has already happened, in Holy Baptism. Jesus has already named you. We are no longer bound by our past or labeled by our infirmities. We are blessed to be a blessing. You are a son or daughter of Abraham. Whatever else we may call you, your name is Christian, child of God. Stand up straight, go in peace, and serve the Lord. Amen.

"Prodigal Son"

Reformation Sunday/October 25, 1998/
Muhlenberg Lutheran Church

LUKE 15:11–32

IN THE FALL OF my junior year at Gettysburg College, I made the Dean's List. Now that is no grand distinction in itself and yet for me, it represented something I had been trying to achieve for the better part of two years. What made this achievement sweeter still was the fact that I had made the Dean's List because I had argued with a professor about a grade. The professor gave me a C on the final exam in philosophy. I had answered the question with my own unique spin of logic and thoughtfulness. When I later challenged him and explained the logic of my answer, he said, "You know I never thought of it that way. You get an A!" It put me over the top and got me on to the Dean's List.

With great excitement I called my folks and told them all about it, "Mom, Dad I made the Dean's List! I aced the Philosophy exam! Bill, Jim, and I are going out to party tonight." My parents replied, "We're proud of you Dean's List or not. Have fun! Be careful!" And party we did. We went to The Pub, a nice little restaurant and college hangout in the middle of Gettysburg, Pennsylvania. I not only learned about philosophy, I also learned about how college students party. You might say we were in the spirit that evening. It was a rollicking good time.

When we closed The Pub down that night and started walking back to campus, it was about 12:15. We were feeling good alright but we weren't loud or boisterous. As the three of us came down through town, we neared the railroad tracks that passed over Carlisle Street. For some reason, the railroad was doing construction, installing a new crossing gate on the street, and there was this ladder that seemed to reach up to the heavens. Now I don't know who started running first, but when the three of us saw the ladder, we knew it was meant to be climbed. And wouldn't you know it, I got there first. I scampered up the ladder and it must have been twenty feet tall. I got almost to the top when I stopped, looked down, and started laughing at my friends. "Hey, give us a turn," Bill yelled. Then I noticed a white car had pulled up to the curb, an officer stepped out, and my friends backed away. I stopped laughing and slid down the ladder. You know the impulse; run like hell. The officer, however, meant business. He slapped his hand on his night-stick, took a step toward me, and said, "Don't try and run punk!" I froze like a scared rabbit. While the officer took me by the arm and led me to the police car, he told my friends to beat it. He put me in the back seat, locked the door, and proceeded to the station. Now I was scared stiff but unfortunately, I chose not to keep my mouth shut, the product of too many TV police dramas. I demanded "Aren't you going to read me my rights?" I was pre-Seminary not pre-Law. When we got to the station, the officer wrote me up and handed me the ticket and the summons to appear in court. Mr. Dean's List had to call home that night, and sobbing on the phone, I told my parents how I had been arrested. "Well Joe, you've had quite a day. We love you Dean's List or not, disorderly and in jail or not! Try to get some sleep. We are glad you are okay and not hurt. We'll come and have breakfast first thing in the morning."

That day I learned a lot about myself but, more importantly, I learned about the nature of grace and unconditional love. My parents were a font of pure grace and forgiveness. I, who had been so busy trying to impress and make my mark, flushed and proud with the excitement of my success, had, in a quick foolish college prank, crashed down. Dean's List in the morning and, college punk that night. I was brought down to earth because I had climbed too high and it was a humbling experience. But more than that, I tell you, it was the grace and forgiveness of my parents who loved me, whether I was on the Dean's List or a disorderly college punk.

Now we all live in a world that measures our behavior and performance. From job performance and academic grades, to our behavior on the street to behind the wheel of an automobile, our performance and behavior is measured and recorded again and again. Progress is charted as well as a record of our failures. At the level of our personal relationships, we also have expectations. How we act with each other makes a difference in all of our relationships.

Things weren't much different in Martin Luther's day. Somehow it all came back to behavior and performance, parents with high expectations, the state with the law ready to punish evildoers, and the church which taught that God was keeping a list of right and wrong, and that one's final destiny depended on behavior. God was the Divine Judge seated on the rainbow of heaven with a balance in his hand, weighing good and evil. Luther tried his best to live within the system. While Luther disappointed his parents by becoming a monk, he tried his best to please God, but he never felt like he had done enough and so plagued was he with his own performance. Finally, after long years of struggle and reading Scripture, Luther experienced the grace of God when he realized there was nothing he could do to make a difference with God. The good news of St. Paul proclaimed, "all have sinned and fallen short of the glory of God, they are now justified by his grace as a gift in Jesus Christ." (Romans 3:23) God already forgave, loved, and accepted him because of Jesus' death and resurrection. Now, God was no longer an angry judge but the one who comes to meet us where we are, sinners in need of grace and forgiveness as well as anxious over-achievers trying our best to impress God.

Luther got in touch with the grace of God found in Luke, chapter 15. The Loving Father forgives the Prodigal who returns home from the pigpen and refuses to be impressed with the goodness of the older brother. God is not impressed with our goodness. God has enough of his own. God is bigger than all our badness, forgiving our sin and calling us to new life. In this world of grades and laws, behavior and performance, standards and high expectations, isn't it wonderful to know where we are loved and forgiven, welcomed home, and given a new start? As the hymn proclaims, "Amazing Grace, how sweet the sound that saved a wretch like me,"[1] for Dean's List students and lawbreaker punks, for anxious monks, and for you and me. Amen.

---

1. "Amazing Grace, How Sweet the Sound" *Hymn #779* John Newton, Evangelical Lutheran Worship, Augsburg Fortress, Minneapolis, 2006.

"Billy Burns"

St. Simon & St. Jude/October 28, 2019/
The National Cathedral

JOHN 15:17–27

IT IS A JOY to be a chaplain at The National Cathedral and to preach and preside at Eucharist. And as the cathedral follows an appointed calendar of Scripture readings for the church year, it has been a surprise for me to preach quite a few festivals and saints' days. As I receive my assignments, I am grateful for notations in the calendar. For St. Mary Magdalene and St. Matthias, the note behind their names read, "Apostles," to tell me they were messengers of the gospel. I never heard of Thecla of Iconium, but learned she became a Christian after hearing St. Paul preach. The note behind her name read, "Proto-martyr among women," telling me she gave her life for the gospel. It is good to remember the saints.

St. Paul tells us, "We carry this treasure in earthen vessels." (2 Cor 4:7f). In consulting the calendar and readings for today, we have St. Simon and St. Jude, with a note behind their names reading, "Apostles and everybody." Apostles I understand. St. Simon and St. Jude are mentioned in the list of Jesus' disciples in the Gospels, but what does "everybody" mean? Having read as much as I could, one article put it bluntly: "These two are the least well-known of the Apostles. Simon, sometimes called the Zealot, may have been a member of a Jewish revolutionary sect. While Jude, whose name is like Judas, was never thought of very highly and never prayed to except as a last resort. St. Jude is referred to as the "saint of lost causes. There is little we know about them."[1]

So now I understand what "everybody" means. Who are the saints? They aren't extraordinary people, although they can be. No, they are ordinary people, loved by Jesus to share the good news. In our Gospel, Jesus says, "I am giving you these commands so you may love one another. If the world hates you, be aware it hated me before it hated you. If you belonged to the world, the world would love you as its own. Because you do not belong to the world, but I have chosen you, therefore the world hates you. Servants are not greater than their master. If they persecuted me, they will persecute you; if they kept my word, they will keep yours also." (John 15:17–20) Saints, as someone has said, are not extraordinary people but ordinary people in the hands of an extraordinary God. I believe every town, church, and community has people who may be gifted and great, yet also quite humble and different, even strange.

Let me tell you about one of them. In the little Pennsylvania town where I grew up, Billy Burns was a kind of misfit. He went to school but wasn't very bright and because he didn't drive, he walked everywhere. You could see him pulling his wagon to the grocery store and back home again. His route would take him down our street. He had thick glasses, a red ruddy face, and he limped when he walked. I know we made fun of him but Billy was kind. He would laugh and wave and was a very gentle soul. My dad and Billy were in high school together and he told me how Billy made an impact on him. Whenever the people of God gathered for worship, Billy Burns was there. He would sing the hymns because he knew them by heart. But when Billy sang, he was always a half beat behind everyone else and he didn't sing softly. He sang out because he loved church and he knew Jesus loved him.

Another story got my attention. When my dad and Billy went to high school, there was a yearly Civics test on the United Nations. Students with high scores were given an all-expense-paid trip to the United Nations in New York City. The class valedictorian won, another student came in second, and coming in third was Billy Burns.

1. *Lesser Feasts and Fasts 2018*, Copyright 2019, The Church Pension Fund. Used by permission. All rights reserved.

The principal was shocked. How could Billy Burns win? They called him into the office, accused him of cheating, and stripped him of the prize. When the students found out what happened, they went to see Billy at his unkept home on the edge of town. When they walked into his room, they were stunned to see the walls covered with articles, posters, pictures, and information about the United Nations. The students returned to the principal, lobbied for Billy to make the trip to New York to visit the United Nations, and he did.

Who are the saints? They aren't extraordinary people. They are ordinary people like Billy Burns and you and me, but they have a hope and a faith that animates them and shines through. And what is this hope and faith? First John tells us, "See what love the Father has given us, that we should be called children of God and that is what we are." (1 John 3:1) We don't know much about St. Simon and St. Jude. We know they were Apostles and they stand for everybody, including all the saints, the people like you and me and Billy Burns. If they misunderstood Jesus, who are we to think we will be any different? So, we limp and struggle just like Billy to let our lights shine, share our gifts, and make our small contributions. In the end, it is not our greatness that makes a difference but the love of Jesus who blesses us to become children of God. Jesus says "Blessed are you poor in spirit, you who mourn, blessed are the meek, the merciful, the pure in heart, those who hunger and thirst for righteousness. . . " (Matthew 5:3–6)

In the end of it all, the race is not to the strong and the swift, but for each of us to bear the treasure of God's good news, sing our songs, run our race, and give thanks to God and all those who have encouraged us. It is for us to encourage others to let their lights shine too. We are all unique, different, and strange but it is the love of Jesus who makes us what we are. This is our hope and faith, in the words of First John's epistle: "Beloved we are God's children now, what we will be has not yet been revealed. What we do know is this: when He is revealed we will be like Him, for we will see Him as he is." (1 John 3:2) Amen.

"Life, Stuff, and True Riches"

Pentecost Season/August 5, 2007/
Muhlenberg Lutheran Church

LUKE 12:13–21

As I THINK BACK on it, I was about ten years old. My mom's mom died of cancer, and a few years later my grandpa remarried. Grandpa and his second wife had a happy marriage but after about seven years together, he eventually became ill and died. Several weeks after his funeral and the reading of the will, which gave directions about the major assets, the whole family got together at my grandparents' home and divided up the remaining furniture and family heirlooms. Now this was their home in the country where I had been thousands of times and where my sister and I often stayed overnight. Every Saturday evening, we would watch *Bonanza* with my grandparents and after that, we would eat Breyer's ice cream and watch *Lawrence Welk*. We ate Sunday dinner there every week after church. I remember grandma's great fried chicken and the iced tea in the large glass pitcher. After lunch we would take long walks in the country with my grandparents, picking raspberries and playing in the yard. It was a great place for kids and my grandparents were wonderful and loving.

On that particular day of dividing things, my grandparents' home looked like it had been looted. Furniture and family heirlooms were spread out all over the yard, as my mom and her two brothers walked among it all. Mom got my grandma's marble-topped vanity dresser and my uncle got the cedar chest, while my other uncle got the gun rack. When it came to the cherry rocker and the antique Pennsylvania rifle, my mom and her brother couldn't agree. So, they asked my dad to flip a coin. Mom got the rifle and my uncle got the rocker. It went on like this for several hours. I don't remember any fights but there were some tense moments and a few more coin tosses. By the end of the day, the house stood empty and forlorn as all of my grandparent's possessions were divvied up and hauled away in pickup trucks.

In our Gospel, Jesus and his disciples are making their way toward Jerusalem when someone asks him to mediate a dispute. Back then, just as it is now, inheritance and the management of estates after the death of parents could be a conflicted affair for children. Jesus refuses to get involved. Instead, he issues a warning and proclaims, "one's life does not consist in the abundance of possessions." (Luke 12:15)

Jesus' parable is told to the man making the request as well as the crowds and disciples who gather to listen, "The land of a rich man produced plentifully . . ." (Luke 12:16) The first truth is that it is God's creation. The land is fruitful! Those who are wealthy often forget in the midst of their self-congratulatory boasting about hard work and ingenuity, that God is always first and foremost the giver of all life's gifts. But let's give the rich man his due. Maybe he worked hard and was a good steward of his resources. He is conservative and careful, one we might admire as a wise and successful businessman.

But God said to him "Fool!" (Luke 12:20) and a judgment is rendered over his life because he is all wrapped up in himself. He lives for himself. He talks to himself. He plans for himself. He even congratulates himself. We hear nothing of family, friends, or his neighbors. He is a fool because he has no thought for others, no thought or regard for God who has given him all the riches he calls his own, but he is making plans and preparations. He's got it all figured out, as if to say, "Gonna pull down those barns and build bigger ones!"

Now we may not be so foolish. I think many of us give thanks to God for life and all of our blessings, but let's face it, we can become addicted to things. Have you heard comedian George Carlin's routine about stuff? "Everybody's got stuff. This is my stuff, that's your stuff. That's all your house is: a place to keep your stuff. If you didn't have so much stuff, you wouldn't need a house. You could just walk around all the time. A house is just a pile of stuff with a cover on it. You can see that when you're in an airplane. You look down, you see little piles of stuff. And when you leave your house, you gotta lock it up. Wouldn't want somebody to come by and take your stuff. That's what your house is, a place to keep your stuff while you go out and get more stuff! Sometimes you gotta move, gotta get a bigger house. Why? No more room for your stuff!"[1]

I think we can identify with bigger barns too, because we like big stuff! We have Big Gulps. We're into big-box stores like Big Lots, Wal-Mart, big bookstores and bulk buying like Costco. Why buy the four-pack of toilet paper when you can buy the big bundle of twenty-four rolls of toilet paper?! We watch big-screen TVs. And why have a little grill when you can buy the big stainless-steel model? We like Big and we like our stuff.

Like Scrooge in "*A Christmas Carol*," the joke is on the rich man in our Gospel because God and Death come calling. God asks the haunting question: "The things you have prepared whose will they be?" (Luke 12:20). My mom still has the marble-top vanity dresser, the rifle, and other things from my grandparents. I don't know if my uncles still have their stuff. But you know what? Little by little it is all being scattered to the wind.

The rich man is shocked, but it does not have to be so with us. Jesus gives bad news to all who store up treasures. The preacher of Ecclesiastes declares, Life is ". . . vanity of vanities, what do we get by all the toil under the sun?" (Ecclesiastes 1:2–3) Jesus is calling us to rethink and reorient our lives. The truth is the death rate is still 100 percent and we don't get to keep anything! How shall we live a life that is rich toward God? Paul says, "If we have been raised with Christ, seek the things that are above, not on things that are on earth." (Colossians 3:1)

Lest we become fools, it is good to keep our death in mind as an incentive to live well each day as it may be our last. Jesus taught

1. "A Place for My Stuff" Studio Album by George Carlin, Atlantic Records, 1981.

us to pray for daily bread, to value people rather than things, and to forgive as a way of healing. Could it be that our relationships and daily bread are enough? The saddest part of the parable is that, for all we know, the rich man had none of the joy of giving or the satisfaction of sharing his riches.

Have you made a will? Do you want your kids fighting over stuff when you die? And when you do make a will, don't leave it all to your children, but give some away to a good cause such as the church. We are never more godly than when we give our lives away. I remember that day of dividing up my grandparents' stuff, but what I cherish is the time and love I shared with them. I get to keep that. That is eternal.

Jesus tells this parable as he goes to Jerusalem. He travels light. His labor, his joy, and his greatest passion is to give his life away for others through Love. May God's Spirit teach us to number our days that we may follow Jesus' way of wisdom, gratitude, and generosity. "For what profit would it be for us if we gain the whole world and forfeit our lives?" (Mark 8:36) Amen.

"Offensive Good News"

2007/Arlington, Virginia/National Workshop on Christian Unity

LUKE 4:14–30

IT WAS A STRANGE encounter, and one of those moments quite frankly where I wanted just to disappear and get away from my family. It was several years ago now and we were all gathered around the table for Christmas dinner at my parents' home. My father's aunt Edna and uncle Herbert were there, dear people who had given my father money to attend seminary, had always been so kind and generous toward me as well. We were doing what families do at such gatherings. We were telling stories, remembering the past, and reminiscing about our lives together. If you've ever been at such a family event, you know that you are never safe and that someone is inevitably going to trot out a story or two about you. Aunt Edna and Uncle Herbert had been regaling all of us with tales about my dad and life on the farm, and it was all a nice trip down memory lane and through Vought family history, when Aunt Edna started to gush all over me. "Oh Joey, you were always such a good boy. You and your sister were always so polite when you would come to visit. Remember how you used to imitate your dad, by getting up on that tree stump outside your grandmother's house and preaching to all the neighborhood children. What beautiful children you have! How is your church work? We hear your congregation in Richmond is growing! We're so proud of you!" At this point, I'm sitting there smiling, trying to be a good sport while Aunt Edna is on a roll.

It would have been fine if it had just ended there, but my dad opened his mouth, "Why don't you tell them what you've been up to lately. Tell them about your special parishioners." Then I began to tell them just a little bit about my visits to Death Row in Virginia and how I had been called to go there to visit a relative of one of my parishioners, and that I'd begun visiting one day a month, with all of the men on Death Row. The warm, loving smiles faded, jaws dropped, and looks of disbelief spread over their faces. Aunt Edna was heard to say, "Well. I think they should be put to death! They certainly deserve what they get. You're ministering to them?!" My mother, realizing this lovely Christmas dinner was about to turn cold and nasty, piped up, "Well, who's ready for some Christmas cookies and dessert? And look at all those presents under the tree! We've got gifts to unwrap!"

So, I think I have a little understanding of what happened to Jesus in Nazareth when pride over the hometown boy turned nasty. Jesus had finished reading Isaiah the prophet and preached a great little homily. "All spoke well of him and were amazed at his gracious words. Is not this Joseph's son?" (Luke 4:22) Can you imagine the people gushing, "Yeah, little Jesus, remember him running through the streets, following his daddy, the carpenter?" Jesus surprises the hometown crowd not because he preaches a great homily, but because he does not keep with family tradition to follow in his father's footsteps, but instead dares to proclaim himself God's messenger.

Now that was perhaps shock enough for the folks in Nazareth, and it would have been enough for Jesus to stop there and just leave them wondering. The homily was good and it would have been better had Jesus just pronounced the benediction, said Amen, and sat down, but he keeps going. Jesus ignites their anger and rage when he dares to suggest that the good news of God to the poor, release of the captives, recovery of sight to the blind, and freedom for those oppressed is not just for those in Nazareth and Judaism, but for outsiders and those beyond the boundaries of Judaism. By calling to mind the widow of Zarephath and Naaman the Syrian, Jesus is clearly saying that, just as God's grace and healing once came to these outsiders, his own ministry will do the same. You can almost hear Aunt Edna and the hometown crowd saying, "You're ministering to them?!"

For all of his advice about winning friends and influencing people, Dale Carnegie is very much a realist when he reminds us, "When dealing with people, remember you are not dealing with creatures of logic, but with creatures of emotion, creatures bristling with prejudice and motivated by pride and vanity."[1] We rejoice to receive the Gospel for ourselves, but then when we realize the full implications, that God loves sinners, accepts them, and forgives them, including those we think haven't quite measured up, we get downright offended.

You want another story? Take a look at Jonah. Jesus could have referenced the Ninevites as well as the widow of Zerapheth and Naaman the Syrian. When the pagan people of Nineveh repented and God spared their city, Jonah went storming off into the desert and prayed an angry prayer to God, "O Lord, is not this what I said while I was still in my country? That is why I fled to Tarshish at the beginning; for I knew that you are a gracious God and merciful, slow to anger and abounding in steadfast love, and relenting from disaster." (Jonah 4:2)

Isn't it curious? We want good news of God's love and forgiveness for ourselves and those we love, but we are just as content to mete out correction and God's justice for others? If the good news of God's love to this human creation is only good news for some, then it is not good news; it is bad news.

By the end of the Gospel today, we perceive the hometown crowd of Nazareth are the ones who are judged and the outsiders are blessed. It is Jesus' favorite way of telling the good news in Luke's Gospel: like the story of two men who went up to pray in the temple, one a Pharisee, full of pride and in need of repentance, while a repentant tax collector is the one who receives grace. Or the story of a father with two sons, one who is lost and wants to earn his way back into the father's good graces, and one who thinks his younger brother ought to get what's coming to him, and that, for

1. "How To Win Friends and Influence People" by Dale Carnegie, 1936, CC-BY-SA license.

his part, he's been a good boy and deserves a reward. What both boys discover, much to their shock and amazement, is that it's not about them. It's about a loving father who welcomes his children to a party because they are his children and he loves them.

It seems to me that our praying and working for church unity is as much about speaking the word of truth and yes, judgment to our own traditions (speaking to the prejudices and stereotypes we carry) as much as it is meeting one another in ecumenical gatherings. Of course, we all live with stereotypes and we may even use them in humorous ways to illuminate our own prejudices and teach others. I remember Bishop Frank Vest of the Episcopal Diocese of Southern Virginia commenting at a conference about his affection for Lutherans, "Oh we always appreciated you Lutherans. You settled the Shenandoah Valley, providing a nice buffer between us and the Indians on the frontier." More than that, I have very fond memories of that dear man who spoke the truth in love and lived the Gospel when he met me at Greensville Correctional Center after I had walked with, and ministered to, a man on Death Row who was executed. Bishop Vest stood in that field and he prayed for all of us in our moment of need.

We are not baptized, called, and ordained to tend the denominational store and the religious franchise. We are called to proclaim the good news, to let the good news of God's redeeming grace have free course, to be children of the light, and to bring this light to the dark places. We do not have God in our back pocket. God will not be manipulated or domesticated. With God there is no hometown favorite, most favored national status, or denomination. Those who speak the truth in love, pray and work for the unity of God's church and the reunion of this lost creation are really like the wise men in T.S. Eliot's poem, "The Journey of the Magi." "We have been to the Manger and worshiped the Newborn King. We have seen this Light to the nations and we go home by another road, where we are never quite at home in the old kingdoms."[2]

God is a God of love and grace for all of this lost human creation. This God will change us because our Lord aims for nothing

2. "The Journey of the Magi" by T.S. Eliot. Collected Poems 1909–1962, Faber & Faber Ltd, 1974.

less than our total conversion. This God may confound you, and call to himself people you wouldn't be caught dead with. The amazing thing is God dares to do even that: Jesus goes his way and not ours. He goes all the way to Death Row, strung up between a repentant and unrepentant thief, and dares to say, "Today you will be with me in paradise." (Luke 23:43)

Thank God it's amazing grace, because our God aims at nothing less than a new creation. In the name of the Father and of the Son and of the Holy Spirit. Amen.

"Simple Things, Great Love"

Maundy Thursday/April 8, 2004/ Muhlenberg Lutheran Church

JOHN 13:1–7, 31–35

WE LIVE IN A world of violence and despair. On this Holy Thursday, we are only too aware of the dreadful conflict in the Middle East that puts lives in peril in a faraway land with no easy way out. A quick scan of the headlines in recent days recalls the genocide in Rwanda ten years ago, where 800,000 people perished in tribal bloodshed while a world stood paralyzed and watching. A new monument will soon be opened to the public in Washington, DC that will commemorate World War II, when another generation had to confront evil on a monstrous scale, lives were lost, and our world was changed.

Confronted with evil and violence on such a grand scale we often become paralyzed as individuals with the enormity of it all. What can any one person do when confronted with evil? How can we ever hope to live well in a violent world? We may never be able to do anything, as individuals, to turn the tide of human bloodshed and the holocausts that have been visited upon the human family. They will no doubt continue as long as this world rolls on. But the story of our salvation tells us that it is not about the big plays or grand campaigns, but it is all about a kind of courage and godly grace in one person who not only confronts the evil but changes the world with one simple act. The sages have taught us that by one act of kindness, a whole new world may be created. When we witness or learn of such acts of courage, we do well to share them with others.

One of my favorite stories about a small act that changed the world was in the early days of Reconstruction following the Civil War in Richmond, Virginia. At St. Paul's Episcopal Church one Sunday morning, a black man presented himself at the altar rail to receive Holy Communion. Now up to that point, only white people were allowed at the altar rail in the nave to receive communion. Black folks were restricted to the balcony. Seeing the black man at the rail, the congregation was silent, the priests stood still, unsure, watching and waiting. All of a sudden, from out of the congregation, there walked a distinguished gentleman in a gray suit who stood beside the black man to receive Holy Communion. His name was General Robert E. Lee.[1]

A similar story is told about Jackie Robinson, the first black player in baseball. He was jeered at, spit upon, spiked intentionally by opposing players, and repeatedly ridiculed for being in the game. In one particular game in Cincinnati, the crowd was especially violent and vulgar, heaping insults and throwing things at Robinson while he was on the field. In the middle of the melee, Pee Wee Reese walked over to Jackie Robinson, stood beside him, and simply put his arm around him. Then, his whole team rose up, walked out of the dugout, and shook his hand. The crowd fell silent with shame, and that is when the whole climate began to change.[2]

This is the way the world is healed. St Paul reminds us that we have the capacity within us to unleash human terror and pain, as well as to bless and to give life. "By one man's disobedience, the sin of Adam, we were all made sinners, and by one man's act of obedience, Jesus Christ, we all were made righteous." (Romans 5:19)

As we enter the great three days of Holy Week (Maundy Thursday, Good Friday, and Holy Saturday) we pause as if on a threshold to see Jesus in the last great acts of ministry doing simple

1. Jay Wink "What John Kelly Got Right About Robert E. Lee" November 3, 2017 The Wall Street Journal.

2. Brian Cronin, "Did Reese really embrace Robinson in '47" April 13, 2013 ESPN.com

deeds of love and kindness, mercy, and forgiveness. On the night of his betrayal, when fear is all around, and the death plot of Judas has already been hatched, Jesus does not do a mighty miracle. He does not call down legions of angels from heaven. He does not convert the traitor Judas, nor does he give courage to Peter, the one who will deny him. On this night, our Lord Jesus shows us love's true measure. He does a few simple things with great love. He celebrates a meal with his disciples. He breaks the bread of forgiveness and lifts a cup of salvation with one who would betray him, one who would deny him three times, and those who would forsake him and run. And then, mindful of the path that he must walk, the Stations of the Cross before him, Our Lord Jesus takes off his outer garment, girds himself with a towel, and stoops to wash the very feet of those who would turn and run away from him, leaving him to die on the cross.

When it happened, those disciples couldn't understand it all, simple acts done with such great love and kindness, even when he told them what it was all about: "I give you a new commandment, that you love one another. Just as I have loved you, you also should love one another." (John 13:34) But all the way through the Passion, through that terrible Friday and that long dark Saturday, he was with them. He was with those feet he had washed, as his body and blood coursed through their veins. They could never run away from him if they tried. And, after the Passion, in the new light of Easter, those simple acts would become their way of remembering, of learning to live like Jesus and follow his example.

This is the way the world is healed. When we gather in his name, we proclaim his life, death, and resurrection until he comes again. This is how we live in a violent world. We live in the breaking of the bread and the lifting of the cup, in the washing and the serving, and in the Lord lifted up. We many never really be able to do great things, but with Jesus, all we really need to do is the small things with great love. Amen.

"Wisdom in the Wilderness"

Advent Season/December 6, 2020/
Abiding Presence Lutheran Church

Isaiah 40:1–11; Mark 1:1–8

Today we have a big word in our Scripture readings for Advent: Wilderness! We are waiting for God in the midst of deprivation, testing our souls, our faith, our country, our world through a time of wilderness and disease. But guess what? We are not the first.

Why did all the people of Judea and Jerusalem go streaming into the wilderness to be baptized by John the Baptist? Because God's people have always been led into the wilderness to be called and shaped by God. Abraham and Sarah were barren and wandered in faith for years till God blessed them with Isaac. Jacob wrestled in the wilderness and came out blessed and limping with God's promise. Moses fled to the desert as a fugitive, only to be called by God to shepherd Israel. The Children of Israel came out of Egypt into the desert where God gave them the law and it took them forty years to enter the Land of Promise. David fled from a murderous King Saul, hardened in the desert, singing Psalms of deliverance, relying on God before becoming king. Ezekiel stood in a valley of dry bones asking God if the bones could live. Now, Isaiah cries "Comfort my people," giving hope to God's people in the wilderness.

So, it was in the days before Jesus, the worship of God in the temple corrupt, the leaders of Israel unjust, the poor marginalized and the way of God unclear. John the Baptist came crying out, "Prepare the way of the Lord, make his paths straight." (Mark 1:3) Mark says "the whole countryside and Jerusalem went out to the desert to be baptized, confessing their sins" for God's new life. Even in the early days of Christianity, there arose a group called the Desert Fathers who sought God in the wilderness. Listen to their wisdom: "Beguiling and deceptive is the life of the world, fruitless its labor, perilous its delight, poor its riches, delusive its honors; and woe to those who hope in its seeming goods: because of this many die without repentance. Blessed are those who depart from the world and its desires."[1]

God knows we need desert times and wilderness. I am not saying we have to like them, but sooner or later our own lives and self-sufficiency will no longer work. We confess at every worship service. "We have sinned by what we've done and left undone." Translation: There is a God and we are not God! The wilderness is any place or time where we meet our limits and vulnerability. We have to turn to, or learn and look to God for a new start. We are living through a wilderness during this pandemic and it is exposing more suffering than we could have imagined, not just physical disease but economic dislocation, political turmoil, and racial strife. We realize in the wilderness that we need God and others. So, when is the last time you met your limits and you had to trust God or others to be born again?

In my senior year of college, I spent January on an adventure called Outward Bound, a month-long course of winter-mountain survival in the Great Smoky Mountains of North Carolina where the average daily temperature was twenty degrees. We were thrown together with people we had never met. My group consisted of three college students, two businessmen, a teacher, a housewife, and a CEO. We spent a week training with our counselors including subjects such as orienteering, map reading, winter survival, hypothermia drills, first aid, making camp, and cooking. We spent three days spelunking in a cave and each of us did three days alone in the woods. The final test was our eight-person mountain trek over thirty miles of wilderness without the aid of our counselors. Did we

1. Elder Nazarius, "Wisdom from the Desert Fathers" https://orthodoxwiki .org › Uncategorized Quotes

remember our training, would we work as a team, and care for each other? At one point we got totally lost and we were dog-tired. That evening, we pitched our tents near the top of a mountain. We awoke to two feet of snow with one person with symptoms of hypothermia which meant we had to strip them nearly naked, throw them in sleeping bag with two others, and raise their core body temperature. We argued about which way to go. We were totally exhausted and it was all pretty scary until we all agreed we were going to stop the panic, keep the faith, use our brains, and get through this wilderness test as a group.

Brene Brown, a social scientist who has written on vulnerability and courage, reminds us, "We are hard-wired for struggle. We are also hard-wired for community."[2] Where in the world is your struggle and where in the world is God leading you? We are all waiting for God this Advent, in a time of pandemic, wilderness, and deprivation. The great stories of our faith and the lives of the saints and history tells us we are not the first to travel this path. Being led into the wilderness where we must surrender control or our own ideas to be born again is a fearful thing to ponder, but there is wisdom to be discovered in wilderness places and times. The truth is often revealed in our trials. And wherever two or three are gathered together in God's name or a common endeavor, there is faith, hope, and love for the journey. I love the way I see it happening in this community through the way we challenge and encourage each other. God is with us bringing us through the struggle.

Let me end this homily with Martin Luther's beautiful words on this life and our baptismal journey of faith.

> This life is not righteousness but growth in righteousness.
> Not health, but healing;
> not being, but becoming . . .
> We are not yet what we shall be,
> but we are growing toward it,
> the process is not yet finished
> but it is going on,

2. The Power of Vulnerability by Brene Brown " You're imperfect, and you're wired for struggle, but you are worthy of love and belonging." (brainyquote. com)

this is not the destination –
but it is the road.
All does not yet shine in glory,
but all is being purified.[3]

God of the wilderness and our salvation, not our will but yours be done. Come quickly, make your advent in our lives, show us your salvation, and we shall be healed. In the name of the Father, Son and Holy Spirit. Amen.

3. "Defense and Explanation of All the Articles," Luther's Works, Vol. 32: Career of the Reformer , ed. George Forell and Helmut Lehman, Fortress, 1958. P. 24.

"Wedding Servants"

Epiphany Season/January 20, 2019/
Community Lutheran Church

JOHN 2:1–11

WHEN I READ THE Gospel for today of Jesus' first miracle at Cana, turning water into wine, I remembered the wedding of Mark and Leigh. They were James Madison University students, part of our campus ministry in my former parish in Harrisonburg, Virginia. They attended worship every Sunday and started dating in their junior year of college. In their senior year, they became engaged and asked me to do the wedding. So, after six sessions of pre-marital counseling, conversations about their similarities and differences, vocational goals, family and children, how to disagree and forgive, as well as spirituality and religion, finally we read through the Service of Marriage together. I invited them to select scripture readings, vows, and make other decisions about the ceremony. I was delighted when they asked for Holy Communion. I suggested instead of just watching other people commune, they might be the ones to model servanthood in their marriage by helping to serve communion to the congregation. They readily agreed.

On the day of the wedding, after the homily and the vows, I celebrated Eucharist and after communing Leigh and Mark, they took their places, each with a pouring chalice ready to serve the congregation. As I gave the Body of Christ to each communicant, Leigh and Mark were on either side of me, pouring wine into each person's cup, but then Leigh became quite emotional as she communed her family and friends. She did her best to pour into each cup and not spill a drop on the people but she couldn't stop shaking and the wine was dripping over her hands and onto her bridal gown. She steeled her nerves to keep on serving, smiling and loving every minute of it, but by the end of it all, her white gown had a bright wide river of red and purple wine down the middle. Other brides might have been mortified but Leigh did not care at all. And after communion when I pronounced the benediction over them, Leigh and Mark kissed and they could not have been happier. They took it all in stride and smiled as they processed down the aisle. And then there was another miracle. When Leigh and Mark walked into the reception hall, Leigh's wedding dress was white as snow. She had used a "Tide Stick" and it all came out. My wife exclaimed, "My gosh, we should have filmed a commercial right there for "Tide Sticks!" But more than anything, the love of God had drawn Mark and Leigh together in their marriage and helped them to serve. Surrounded and loved by family and friends, what could shake their joy and happiness? It wasn't about them. They were happy to serve. It was one of the most beautiful memorable weddings in which I presided.

Today Jesus goes to a wedding with his disciples as one of the invited guests. Jesus enjoyed wine and parties, and most of his best parables were about great feasts. When the wine gave out, Jesus gives directions, water is poured, ladled out, and taken to the head waiter. The waiter can't believe the aroma and the sparkle, this drink from God. Celebration!

The one who came from God as a baby in a manger, who is worshiped by Three Kings of the Gentiles, who was baptized and declared God's Son as the Light of Heaven danced on the Jordan River: Jesus, the Word of God who became human, does his first miracle at a wedding with wine because God is married to his people. The spotlight is no longer on the couple but now God's Epiphany light is focused on Jesus. It is the wedding of Heaven and Earth; God marries humanity in Jesus. It is what Isaiah foretold, "The Lord delights in you and your land shall be married. For as a young man marries a woman and rejoices over a bride, so shall your God rejoice over you." (Isaiah 62)

Jesus is the one who keeps the party going even when other people don't have a clue. But Jesus' disciples know and they believe. It is the power and mystery of the Word made Flesh, of one who lives with us, gives up his life that there may be new life. Mark and Leigh knew it wasn't about them. It was all about Jesus in their marriage, helping them to love and serve. Jesus is married to us in our baptism of dying and rising with him so that we may be faithful disciples, listening to his Word and ready to serve. This Spirit of Jesus is celebrated in every marriage when we give ourselves to something bigger than ourselves. It is lived in every congregation where Jesus calls us to become more than we ever could be on our own.

So let us learn to bow and bend, to love one another. For Christ is with us in all that we do. How can we not live, love, serve, and give our lives away as good gifts for others? How can we be more at ease and remember it's not always about us, that we bear the light, we carry the love of Jesus to serve others? God has wedded himself to his people! Let the wine flow and let there be singing and dancing in the aisles. This is the good news for our life together, for our ministry, and this community we are called to serve. Let's keep welcoming all people, building up this church, and sharing the light and love of Jesus. Amen.

"Wit and Witness"

*Lauston Funkhouser Funeral/October 14,
2007/Muhlenberg Lutheran Church*

Psalm 23; Isaiah 25:6–9

I first met Lauston and Gladys Funkhouser in 1997 at the 8:30 worship service. They showed up early at 7:45a.m. "Nice to meet you. How are you this morning?," I said. "Not too good, I have aids! Hearing aids!!" I knew I was in the presence of a character, a unique child of God. To know Lauston was to know a man who delighted in just being himself, with no airs and no pretenses. He didn't take himself too seriously because he knew himself to be a forgiven sinner who could laugh and enjoy life. The amazing grace of God and the love of Jesus made him a child of God in his baptism many years ago at St. Jerome Lutheran Church. With God's promise over his life, that set Lauston free to be himself. He was a good husband and father, a beloved grandfather, and a good friend and neighbor. He was a worker in this community. He made the school buses run for the school children and he was a faithful member of Christ's church.

In a place, by a highway that seems to be going way too fast and busy, Lauston and Gladys lived simply and humbly in their small home, enjoying a life of honest work, dear family and friends. And it didn't get any better than when you stopped by for a visit or just to say hello. There was usually something to eat, and stories to share and people to care about, and a good laugh or two to brighten your day. I remember when Lauston and Gladys invited us out one summer day to pick grapes and get some tomatoes and produce from their large and bountiful garden. We got out of the car, and there was Lauston in his characteristic dress of work boots, overalls, long underwear, a flannel shirt, and an engineer's cap on his head. When he saw me, he took off his cap to shake my hand. I could tell what little hair he had on his head had just been trimmed and cut, so I said, "Good to see you Lauston, looks like you got a haircut!" He took off his cap, ran his hand over his head, and said, "Good to see you Pastor, Naw I didn't get no haircut, El Nino done that!" We had such a great time that day, picking grapes and carryin'on with Lauston and Gladys. Another time, when our youth group came caroling to Lauston and Gladys's place, we sang a few songs and they were polite to listen. Then, they invited all of us into their cozy little home on that cold winter's night for a Christmas feast. Lauston, Gladys, and Mildred and the whole family invited all of us in for food, sandwiches and salads, Christmas cookies and cake, and hot chocolate and coffee. And we almost didn't want to leave for all the fun we had.

Maybe it doesn't get much better than that. To live a life of contentment, good humor, and enjoying people, as Lauston and Gladys enjoyed themselves. I know they had their share of struggles and hard times too, but with characteristic faith they did the best they could with what God gave them. They shared their life together and were thankful for each other, their family, and their friends. I will tell one more church story about Lauston. It was a winter Sunday morning and Lauston came into church cold and shivering. He said to the ushers within earshot of most everyone, "I'm cold this morning, can you sit me between two fat ladies?" I knew Lauston and Gladys as worshipers, two children of God with grace and good humor, because they knew who had given them life, health, and salvation.

We give thanks to God for Lauston, for a life well lived with a godly wit and witness. We can thank God for this good family, for Mildred, a faithful daughter, and Patrick, a grandson and the son that Lauston never had. Together they shared a love of steam engines and were known far and wide for that unique hobby. Patrick said the other day, "Granddad and I had a great time and I just wish we could've thrown the throttle open one more time." We give thanks for the family who gathered around Lauston in his dying and death to show their love and care. Even the family cat got up on the bed to be with him. When I last saw Lauston about a week and a half ago, I thanked him for welcoming me and my family to this community, for being a faithful member of Christ's Church, and for being a child of God with a great sense of humor. We laughed together and we cried and when we realized it would be our last meeting, we let God have the last word, we read Scripture, we shared Holy Communion, we prayed the Lord's prayer and for God's peace that passes understanding.

Lauston didn't have much to say about his funeral, but he did make one request, "Make sure the preacher doesn't try to preach me into heaven." Well dear Lauston, I couldn't do it if I tried because Jesus has already opened his kingdom to all believers. The Kingdom of God and the promise of heaven, Isaiah tells us will be time of no more crying, no more pain, and there will be a great gathering on God's Mountain like a grand homecoming with all kinds of wonderful food and good things to eat, a table spread with good things and cups overflowing. When I hear these promises of God, I imagine a table like Lauston's and Gladys', where there is love and food and enough for all with laughter and joy.

The Good Shepherd of Psalm 23 promises to lead us all the days of our lives. Even through the darkest valley, he will never abandon us but walk beside us. And just when we might be fearful of the shadow of death, we are surprised by God's amazing grace, a table spread before us where a cup overflows and we find ourselves in the house of God. This is our hope and may the Peace of God that passes all understanding keep our hearts and minds on Christ Jesus our Lord. Amen.

"A Fishing Fool"

Epiphany Season/February 8, 2004/
Muhlenberg Lutheran Church

Luke 5:1–11

KEN SUTTON IS A fishing fool. This former parishioner of mine loves to fish so much he would often come to church wearing a fish around his neck. Actually, it was a necktie but the silver scaly appearance of it really made you look twice. Not too many years ago, Ken insisted that my son, Jonathan, and I go fishing with him in his bass boat.

One Saturday afternoon, we found ourselves bobbing up and down in Ken's boat on Swift Creek Reservoir, south of Richmond. Now Ken has got all the tackle anyone could ever want, so we were smartly turned out with the best rods and reels as Ken maneuvered the boat to his favorite spots. We fished for about four hours, Ken schooling us all the way, giving us pointers. The only trouble was by the end of the afternoon Ken and I had only caught a few small sunfish while Jonathan, the seven-year-old, had a stringer full of fish, a couple of nice size perch, a good small-mouth bass, and three scrappy catfish. Ken was a good sport as we got out of the boat and took the stringer of fish home, but of course, I couldn't let it go at that. The next Sunday at church, Jonathan presented Ken with his own stringer loaded with cardboard cut-out fish of many colors and announced to him, "Come follow me and I will make you a fisher of fish."

Ken, the fisherman, got shown-up by a seven-year-old kid. And Peter, the man who had fished that lake for the better part of his life, got shown-up by a country rabbi and preacher named Jesus.

Sometimes we think we know something so well that there is nothing more to learn. We've got it all figured out. If we have worked a certain job for any amount of time, we may think we've mastered it. Same old, same old, we like to say. Just putting in my time. It can work that way with the work we do and the hobbies we pursue, like Peter or my friend Ken thinking, 'I know these waters' or because, we have been around for a while, maybe it's us thinking, 'I know this town. I know that person. I've got them all sized up. I know this church. I know my faith. Ain't nothing new here. I've got it all figured out.'

And then, every once in a while, someone will say something, or something will happen to make us look again, to realize we are not as wise as we think we are. That day by the lake, it was Jesus calling to the fishermen who had worked all night, "Put out into the deep and let your nets down for a catch." (Luke 5:4)

Now you and I know how we feel when someone gives us advice about a subject, they know nothing about. "Hey buddy, mind your own business. I'll show you what to do with this net." It is all the more miraculous that Peter responded, "We have caught nothing. Yet, if you say so, I will let down the nets." (Luke 5:5) Peter listened to the Word of the Lord and obeyed. When he was tired and even when he didn't understand it or see the good of it, Peter listened to Jesus and he obeyed. He didn't follow his instinct; he followed Jesus. And because he let go of his attitude, listened to Jesus, and let down those nets, something miraculous happened.

How is Jesus calling us in our jobs and in our daily living to "put out into deep water and let down our nets?" To look at that problem with new eyes, to seize a new opportunity, to do a new thing, to not take something or someone for granted, to admit that we don't have all the answers?

How might Jesus be calling to us in this ship of the church to "put out into deeper waters and let down our nets?" Could it be to listen to Jesus and do something new? Could it be to make worship a weekly priority, to get into Sunday School or Bible Study? Could it be to get to know some new people, start a new group, invite a friend to church? Could it be to do something new instead of whining and thinking we've got it all figured out? This is a great place to take these risks because God loves us and we have each other.

It is an awesome thing to fall into the hands of the living God. God asks too much. God knows too much. God demands too much. Ask Peter who thought he knew a thing or two. I know why Peter, after catching all those fish, asks Jesus to leave. He knows he is in the grip of someone bigger than he is. Peter comes to realize that he really doesn't know after all. He is not really in control like he thought he was. Peter knows his life must change because God is going to have his way anyway. And God will have his way with each of us.

My friend Ken Sutton will tell you that this is a fish story. It is all about the men who think they know how to fish and, lo and behold, they are the ones who are caught. "Put out into the deep and let down your nets for a catch." (Luke 5:4) Jesus tells the fishermen. "Put out into deeper water. . .. Do not be afraid" is what Jesus is saying to you and me. We have only to listen to Jesus and to follow.

Blessed is the one who realizes they are not as smart as they thought they were and takes a second look at life to see the miraculous. Blessed is the one who takes a risk for Jesus' sake. And blessed is the one who comes to understand that our life and our work is not about the bottom line, it's not about what we know, our level of expertise, or just putting in our time. Our life and calling are to serve a purpose greater than ourselves. It is for Jesus who has caught us and claimed us as his own. He asks nothing more of us than that we love and serve the people who are put in our path so that he may sweep them up, and us into the wide net of his love.

Jesus is calling today. He will be calling to us tomorrow and every day, "Put out into deep water and let down your nets. Do not be afraid." Now do you want to sit there or shall we get busy fishing? Amen.

"Treasure in Heaven"

Pentecost Season/August 9, 1998/
Muhlenberg Lutheran Church

LUKE 12:32–40

MY GRANDFATHER DIED THIS past Thursday morning. I was with him on Wednesday, the last afternoon of his life. My dad and I had picked up Grandpa and his girlfriend from the nursing home and we were sitting in the backyard of my aunt's home drinking iced tea, playing Trivial Pursuit, and singing songs.

My grandfather loved to play games. I can remember going to his home as a child. He would meet us at the door with a pitcher of Kool-Aid and a basket of pretzels, saying "Monopoly is set up on the card table, the train set is in the barn, ping-pong in the backyard, and we've got shuffleboard and soccer to play." He loved to entertain us and all the neighborhood children. My grandmother would go crazy because he was always playing with us kids and did not have time for much adult talk, current events, or more worldly things. He was just a big kid. He loved being with us and relating to us through his games. I think it was also one of the ways he handled his disappointments. He was a trained musician who had studied flute and other woodwinds with one of John Philip Sousa's band members. He played in the orchestra at Radio City Music Hall and always marched in the Macy's Day parade. But there came a time when had to leave his first love of music to work for the Pennsylvania Railroad and provide for his family. To his dying day I think he probably regretted saying "No" when a little known band-leader asked him to join his ensemble. Years later the bandleader and his group became famous and known as Les Brown and his Band of Renown.

So, I feel extraordinarily blessed that I was able to share all those wonderful afternoons of gaming and laughter with my grandfather. And how thankful I am that I took off last Sunday through Wednesday to go and be with him. What a gift, that afternoon in my aunt's backyard with my grandpa, his girlfriend, a song or two, and the games. My granddad was really in ill health and not feeling very well at all in the last few weeks. I think he figured, "Heck, if I can't chase Isabelle around the nursing home or play shuffleboard, what's the use of hanging around?"

Friday afternoon I spoke with my father. He and his brothers and sisters went to the retirement center and began to clean out my grandfather's room. Some took furniture, others claimed gifts they had given, took pictures, and small mementos. My dad and his siblings will have to look over the will, then divide up and settle the estate. I hope there will not be any wrangling or fights. I know they would turn it all over and give it away in a heartbeat if they could play one more game or sing one more song with my grandfather.

So where is the sermon in all of this? Where is the Gospel? Just this: "Do not be afraid, little flock, for it is your Father's good pleasure to give you the Kingdom. . . Make purses for yourselves that do not wear out, an unfailing treasure in heaven." (Luke 12:32–33) In the end, the only gift we have to offer is ourselves.

God has already given us the Kingdom! God has given us our lives and eternal life, the gift of salvation yesterday, today, and tomorrow is secure! So, what do we need to be afraid of? Why do our priorities often seem so confused? Why is it that we deal in all kinds of currency and become consumed with so many things that we neglect the important things in life?

Jesus tells us that the Kingdom is ours! It is the love and worship of God and the love and time we invest in others that makes it what it is all about. He helps us to see that everything else, by comparison, should be given away. Everything else is junk compared to the love and worship of God, the time and investment we make in caring for the neighbor. Money and possessions are of course easier to control and manipulate than relationships. In relationships we must practice patience and give up our need to control. To be in relationships with others means that we must learn to bend, practice forgiveness, and allow for the freedom of another.

Grandpa's death has taught me about the Kingdom and where the unfailing treasure lies. We love God and keep the treasure in heaven by giving our lives away as good gifts to others. The death of those we love and the reminder of our own death is often what we need to help us wake up and come to life. Jesus' parable about the servants waiting for the Master is for those of us who are tempted to try and have it both ways. "You cannot serve God and money." (Matthew 6:24)

So where is your treasure? Take an inventory. If you knew you had but one week to live, how would you reprioritize your wealth and treasure? Would you need to change your will? Spend time with a loved one? Forgive a grudge? Square a debt? Tell your family and friends what they really mean to you? Do some act of kindness for a stranger in need?

I should tell you that we went to the Green Valley Auction on Friday. We had fun. We almost bought an antique mirror. I was amazed at all of the stuff for sale, and all of the bidders coming to buy. But as I left the auction, I couldn't help but think of all the people who once upon a time cared for those things, the faces that looked in those mirrors, the people who ate off that beautiful china, and the little children who reached into those antique cookie jars. What were their lives like? Did they feel fulfilled or were they restless and yearning? Surrounded by possessions, were they rich toward God, satisfied with their marriages, loving their families, and serving others? How did they meet their death?

As I think of all these things, the possessions I have, the words of Jesus and the opportunities I have to give and receive love with family, friends, and even people I do not know, I smile and remember sitting in the backyard with my grandfather, drinking iced tea and playing games. I think I know the treasure Jesus is speaking of and I pray to God to keep it. Amen.

"My Fortress, My Stronghold and Deliverer"

Gene Duane Harris Funeral/January 18, 2019/Community Lutheran Church

Psalm 144

"Blessed be the Lord, my rock, who trains my hands for war, and my fingers for battle; my rock and my fortress, my stronghold and my deliverer, my shield, in whom I take refuge, who subdues the peoples under me.

O Lord, what are human beings that you regard them, or mortals that you think of them? They are like a breath; their days are like a passing shadow.

Bow your heavens, O Lord, and come down; touch the mountains so that they smoke. Make the lightning flash and scatter them; send out your arrows and rout them.

Stretch out your hand from on high; set me free and rescue me from the mighty waters, from the hand of aliens, whose mouths speak lies, and whose right hands are false.

I will sing a new song to you, O God; upon a ten-stringed harp I will play to you, the one who gives victory to kings, who rescues his servant, David. Rescue me from the cruel sword, and deliver me from the hand of aliens, whose mouths speak lies, and whose right hands are false.

May our sons in their youth be like plants full grown, our daughters like corner pillars, cut for the building of a palace. May our barns be filled, with produce of every kind; may our sheep increase by thousands, by tens of thousands in our fields. . . Happy are the people to whom such blessings fall; happy are the people whose God is the Lord." (Ps 144)

We, at Community Lutheran Church, were so very blessed to have met and spent two years with Gene Harris. While we didn't get to know him really well, we caught the measure of the man. I remember the first day he walked into church, tall, slightly stooped, with a firm handshake and a warm smile. Salt of the earth, midwestern, tall and rugged from the heartland in Sioux City, Iowa. We got acquainted and shared our stories. I explained I was from Pennsylvania but I married someone from South Dakota and introduced him to Debra. He said, "Well Pastor Joe, you married well."

While he only attended school through the eighth grade, boy did Gene get an education. In the words of Tom Brokaw's best-selling book, he became part of "The Greatest Generation" and served his country. When I watch *Band of Brothers* or *Saving Private Ryan*, I can't help but think of men like Gene and his character and courage. In 1943, Gene joined General George Patton's third Army in WWII, where as a sergeant, he was decorated with the coveted French Croix de Guerre for bravery, the Presidential Citation, the Combat Infantry Medal, and the Good Conduct Medal. In 1947, he married Joan in Sioux City, Iowa. He became a stepfather to Larry and a father to Cindy. Then it was making marshmallows with Kraft Foods in Indiana, followed by employment with Merle Norman Cosmetics in California and finally returning to Sioux City. In retirement Gene was an active member of St. Mark Lutheran Church in Sioux City, enjoyed gardening, woodworking, and visiting with neighbors and relatives. After years of love and nurture from your parents, you invited Gene to move here in 2016 to live with you and Bob. If Gene ever resented the move east, I never saw it. He was grateful and loved you both.

I visited Gene last week at the nursing home in his comfortable room, surrounded by pictures of his family and WW2 memorabilia. I remember him telling stories of trying to stay warm and sleeping in the numbing cold and fear of winter warfare in Europe. He spoke of friends he had made and lost and then, giving thanks to God, that he made it by the skin of his teeth to come back home to start a new life. He was a faithful member of this parish, here every Sunday, giving thanks for all the chapters of his life, to the God who trained his hands for battle, protected him through warfare, gave him a dear wife and loving family, and work and faith that allowed him to build a home and raise good children.

Many of us will never forget two years ago when a Holocaust survivor came to speak at our church. Gene was in the congregation. At the end of his talk Gene introduced himself as a member of the third infantry, the very unit that had liberated the survivor's camp. And there they stood embracing with tears in their eyes. The survivor said, "You were angels sent from God." Gene leaned close with tears in his eyes and responded, "God was our strength and salvation. The Good Lord brought us through it all. What can shake our faith?"

In the words of another Psalm 139, we can almost hear Gene saying it, "O Lord, you have searched me and known me. You know when I sit down and when I rise up; you discern my thoughts from far away. You search out my path and my lying down, and are acquainted with all my ways. Even before a word is on my tongue, O Lord, you know it completely. Where can I go from your spirit? Where can I flee from your presence? If I ascend to heaven, you are there; if I make my bed in Sheol, you are there. If I take the wings of the morning and settle at the farthest limits of the sea, even there your hand shall lead me, and your right hand shall hold me fast."

Well done, good and faithful servant, enter into the joy of your Master. In the name of the Father and of the Son and of the Holy Spirit. Amen.

"Jesus on our Doorstep"

Christmas Season/Dec. 30, 2007/
Muhlenberg Lutheran Church

MATTHEW 2:13–23

IT WAS CHRISTMAS, 1968. My sister and I were up early like most kids on Christmas morning. We were trying not to wake our parents and yet making just enough noise in the hopes that they would wake up so we could all go downstairs to see what Santa had delivered. As mom and dad began to stir, mom saw my sister and me standing in their bedroom doorway like the adorable little angels that we were. "Okay you two, Merry Christmas, you can go downstairs in a little bit, just give me a chance to get down there, get some breakfast things ready, and turn on the Christmas lights." We jumped on the bed with my dad and waited for mom to invite us downstairs. All of a sudden, we heard a frantic and loud pounding on the front door. My dad sat up and we heard my mom scream, "John get down here! There's someone at the door! There's a man on the front porch and he's bleeding! You kids stay up there!" and before we knew it, my mom was flying up the stairs, corralling my sister and me in their bedroom, while my father went downstairs to investigate.

In the little community where we lived in central Pennsylvania, there was one street that ran through the center of town. Besides the neat two-story homes that lined each side of the street, the only other noteworthy buildings were the fire department and the

Lutheran church where my dad was pastor. We lived next door in the parsonage and everyone in the community knew it. It certainly appeared to be the case that Christmas morning as the man who had been beaten and bloody in a local bar the night before was now on our front doorstep asking for help and sanctuary. He had gotten in a fight with two other men. Now they were looking for him to kill him. My dad spent most of Christmas day trying to get him some medical attention and help. Dad reminded me recently of that Christmas day in 1968. He also recalled the man's name, Hector de Jesus.

Christmas has dawned upon us after the anticipation of Advent, and no sooner have we celebrated it, than we begin to confront the hard realities of our world once more. Much as Hector de Jesus stood on our front porch that Christmas morning, the joy of Jesus' birth seems suddenly overtaken by the cares and suffering of the world. No sooner is the child laid in the manger than we realize there is a price on his head. Plots are hatched, angels have to warn Joseph, and the Holy Family escapes Bethlehem just in time. Herod the Great, who murdered members of his family when he thought they were scheming against him, didn't bat an eyelid at the thought of killing lots of little babies in case one of them was the coming King. So, Joseph, Mary, and Jesus became refugees and fled to Egypt for safety beyond the border of Herod's territory. Even when we learn that Herod died and the Holy Family returned to Israel, another move to Nazareth in Galilee was necessary because of Joseph's fear of another Herod.

I remember asking children in my last parish what was so special about Christmas. One little girl piped up, "Christmas is the day Jesus was born and then on Easter, that's the day we killed him." She almost had it right. While the Creeds tell us Jesus, "was born crucified, died and was buried," Matthew wants us to understand that when God came, he came the whole way down to earth.

He was born in humble circumstances. His family became refugees. They moved around during his early years and settled in a little town called Nazareth. He worked as a carpenter until he was thirty. Then he became an itinerant preacher. He never went to college, never wrote a book, and never held a public office. He never had a family but relied on the hospitality of others. He never traveled far and when he did, he walked. He had no credentials but himself. Public opinion turned against him. His followers ran away. He was turned over to the authorities and went through the mockery of a trial. He was sentenced to death between two thieves. While he was dying, his executioners gambled for the only piece of property he had on earth. His body was laid in a borrowed grave provided by a friend.

If Jesus Christ is only God, then he can never identify with our humanity. And, if Jesus Christ is only just a human being, why then he can never deliver or save us. But Matthew tells us that this down-to-earth God will liberate God's people from oppression and bring light to their darkness. Isaiah says that "He became their savior in all their distress. It was His very presence that saved them, his love and pity . . ." (Isaiah 63:8–9). Hebrews tells us "He had to become like us in every respect, because he suffered, he is able to help those who are being tested." (Hebrews 2:17–18).

While we were ready to celebrate Christmas that morning long ago in 1968, Hector de Jesus stood on our doorstep and reminded us to look for Jesus in all of the world's children's faces, in the suffering, and even in the difficult places. He comes for the little ones, the least, and the lost. He comes for the sick, the shut-in, the dying, for refugees, and those in prison. He comes amid our family problems, in our workaday world, and in our troubled dreams. Because God comes down to earth, builds a bridge to us, embraces our humanity, redeems our sinfulness, and lives with us, we are no longer left to ourselves. Jesus loves us, our lives are lifted up to God, and we have the hope the heaven all because of this down-to-earth God whose love will overcome the world. Amen.

"Baptized into Death and Resurrection"

Baptism of Our Lord/January 8, 2017/
Community Lutheran Church

Matthew 3:13–17

In two short weeks, we have come from Jesus' birth to the Baptism of Our Lord. Jesus grows up quickly in the Gospels. The next time we see him he is standing on the banks of the Jordan for baptism. For Jesus, his baptism is as important as his birth. When Jesus steps into the water he joins himself to our humanity. He is Emmanuel, God so totally with us that he dives all the way in. And if there is any doubt, we learn, in the voice from heaven, who it is who wades into the water and takes on our life, "This is my Son, the Beloved . . ." What we see in this baptism is God's anointing and rejoicing in Jesus, God taking on our life, and diving into the stream of our lives to be with us.

So, when a confirmand or someone may ask, "Why do we baptize?," the answer is because Jesus got baptized and told us to baptize. "Go, make disciples and baptize them in the name of the Father, Son and Holy Spirit." (Mt. 28) This is Jesus' great commission. In the affirmation of baptism and at the beginning of every worship service, we turn and remember who we are as human beings. We are not perfect but given a new birth through water and God's Word to be called God's sons and daughters. In Jesus' baptism, going into the water and rising up to hear he is God's beloved, we see the pattern for his life and our own. Dying and rising is the pattern for our life.

It was one thing for my mom and dad to name me Joseph Mark Vought and rejoice in my birth but it was even more important to take me to a font and have me baptized. What happens once in baptism happens again and again. That's why we must remember it and return to it to think about what is dying and rising in us. Life will change a thousand times over and if you stop and think about your own life, you realize it too. I don't remember the day of my baptism, but my mom and dad told me about it. They brought me to church and introduced me to a much more diverse and expansive family where I learned about Jesus. I don't live with my mom and dad or my sister anymore. The day I moved into college, my dad put his hands on my shoulders and said, "Joe, your mother and I will always love you and this is the next step in your great adventure. We want you to enjoy it, study hard, don't get into too much trouble, and go to church because the family of God is there with grace and good news and you will always be welcome." So, I have grown up with other Christian brothers and sisters in many other congregations who are, and remain, my family. You and I, in this family of God, we keep the faith together.

One of my favorite seminary professors, Eric Gritsch, put it this way, "The real question for Christians is not whether one has had that one glorious born-again experience, be it through a Bible or Spirit or both, but rather whether one is born again and again in the encounter with the Gospel of Christ crucified, in the community where two or three are gathered in Jesus' name."[1]

I know there are people who talk about being born again, but I have been born again and again and again and if you are like me, you must have a sense of change throughout your life. We are baptized children of God who, like Jesus take our life's journey born again and again, dying and rising. What is dying in your life right now? What is being raised up for new life in you? What must we die to as a people of God in this place, this church, to be raised up into the people God wants us to be? Sometimes we will be afraid but

---

1. *Born Againism*: Perspectives on a Movement, Copyright 1982 by Eric W. Gritsch. Fortress Press.

that's why we come together, to hear the Word, share the supper, and find our courage to be godly. We trust that the God who claims us in the beginning is the one who walks with us through life and welcomes us to new life.

So, it was about two weeks ago, I sat at my father's bedside in the last stages of his life and baptismal journey. It was a stream-of-consciousness conversation, even some life review. He talked about how proud he was of my sister and me, and perhaps we could take one more family vacation to Disney World . . . the move from his cottage to the nursing home was tough and all the stuff he worried about and wanted to know what became of, it all just didn't matter.

And then he said, "I think I am ready to be with your mom and maybe I'm a little afraid of dying." I said, "Well dad, who wouldn't be? You haven't been there yet. Do you remember that story of the pastor who asked a dying parishioner what it was like to die?" I told him the story again: "When I was a little boy every day I would play in my backyard. There was a swing set, a sandbox, and all my toys where I was at home. My mom and dad were close and were there when I needed them. It was my world and I loved that place. Then one day my mother came to me and said, 'Tomorrow, you will put on new clothes, you will not play in the yard but you will go to school.' He said, I had heard about school but I had never been there and the thought of leaving home and my backyard scared me and I was frightened. But can you imagine my surprise the next day, when I went to school and saw a bigger playground than I could have ever imagined and more friends to play with. I think dying is like that." My dad smiled through tears and nodded.

My brothers and sisters, let us return again and again to our baptism. For all the changes of life, the dying, and rising, may God give us courage to keep the faith, walk forward, encourage each other, and remember, we are God's children now and forever. In the name of the Father, the Son, and of the Holy Spirit. Amen.

"Healing and Uniting Strangers"

Season of Pentecost/June 28, 2015/
Community Lutheran Church

MARK 5:21–43

JESUS MEETS THE NEEDS of two people in today's Gospel who could not have been more different. One is a leader of the town and synagogue named Jairus and one is a woman who had a hemorrhage for twelve years. There are so many ways we are estranged from one another, strangers to those we know and do not know. Illness keeps us from the life we are meant to enjoy and prejudice and fear can blind us. For all of his power and status, Jairus was in need because his little daughter was ill and dying. And all the power and status in the world isn't worth a fig when a loved one lays dying. The woman with the hemorrhage doesn't have a name and maybe that's the way people knew her, for she would have been ritually unclean with such a chronic condition. We don't know if she had any relatives and no one interceded for her. If the town's folk knew of her illness, she was likely ostracized and had to suffer alone. We are told that she suffered and was under many physicians 'cares for years.

There is so much fear in our lives. Disease is a fearsome thing because for all of our knowledge, it seizes us and robs us and makes us strangers to ourselves and to each other. The events of Charleston and too many acts of violence seem to have seized this country like a disease and we wonder about our own healing in this nation. But we are all human beings, made in the image of God and we are all trying to grow up and overcome the things that hold us back, to become the people God wants us to be. A wise man once said, "Be kind and generous, everyone you meet is fighting a great battle."[1] If we ever forget our common humanity, that we are more alike than different, it's not long until we become suspicious, estranged from each other, and begin to hate or hurt.

Jack Nicholson and Morgan Freeman could not have been more different in the 2007 movie, "The Bucket List," where they were thrown together, a black man and a white from different worlds. What they had in common was that both were old cranky men and bigots forced to room together in a hospital because of serious illness. While their initial meetings were hostile, over time they grew to appreciate and support one another, finally becoming the dearest of friends. Sometimes it takes adversity to soften us, to awaken in us compassion and understanding.

In a 2016 visit to Rwanda, a land that bore so much suffering and genocide, we learned of godly acts of courage and compassion in the midst of the violence. In the closing days of the genocide of 1994 when one million people were killed in 100 days from tribal prejudice and violence fanned by colonial powers, Hutu killers arrived in a small western village of Nyange and barged into a school. The murderers ordered the children and the teachers, "All you Tutsis, step out and line up against the wall." There was silence until one girl stepped out and proclaimed, "There are no Tutsis or Hutus here, for we are all Rwandans!" And with that they all died together, proclaiming their common humanity, sharing the death of martyrs, much like those who died for civil rights in our country.

So how do we heal? How do we become agents of healing in a world beset by illness, fear, and prejudice? If we only act out of our own pain and struggle, we become part of the problem and we may easily succumb to hatred and violence. But when we begin to look on a brother or sister who is struggling and remember our common humanity, that here is also one who is loved by God, we begin to chase away the demons of illness, fear, and hatred.

---

1. Philo of Alexandria, goodreads.com/quotes/31538-be-kind-for-everyone -you-meet-is-fighting-a-great-battle

For Jesus who walked and served with the love of God, he touches Jairus and the unnamed woman and both are healed. I'd like to think that Jairus and his daughter, who was healed, and that unnamed woman, cured of her disease, met each other and became friends that day because of Jesus. Today in Rwanda, Hutus and Tutsis continue the healing of that beautiful land and people. One of the powerful ways they do that is to dance together- Hutus and Tutsis-the native dances of their one tribal history. In the words of today's psalm, "You have turned my wailing into dancing." (Ps 30) So maybe Rwanda is a parable of racial ethnic healing that we may come to learn and emulate in our country.

Wherever you go this week, may you look on all the people you meet with new eyes, an open heart, and the kindness of God. May the one who came to bear our humanity, forgive our sins, and heal us of our illness and prejudice, raise us up to be agents of healing and God's peace. And may the peace of God that passes all understanding keep our hearts and minds in Christ Jesus our Lord. Amen.

"A Bridge of Forgiveness"

Pentecost Season/September 7, 2008/
Muhlenberg Lutheran

MATTHEW 18:15–20

JESUS UNDERSTOOD THAT IT is not easy living in relationships with others. He was realistic about conflict because He came from a people whose history was littered with stories of conflict, family feuds and forgiveness: Cain who murdered Abel; two feuding brothers Jacob and Esau; Joseph who was sold into slavery by his brothers; and a story Jesus told about a younger brother who ran away with the family inheritance and the elder brother who stayed home and a Loving Father who wanted both of them to forgive each other.

The prevailing idea about conflict throughout much of the Bible and in our culture is the idea of retribution: you get what you deserve, "an eye for an eye." It is no wonder that we don't manage our conflicts well. We either escalate conflict and demonize the other, OR we distance ourselves and we shun the offender. It happens between nations, in communities, in families and in the church. Someone does something that offends us, and instead of saying something we nurse the grudge. And then because a relationship is strained and we imagine that the other person knows what they did and should really apologize to us, it causes our stomach to churn and keeps us up at night. We know we need to let it out, but instead of going to the person who offends us, we talk to other people and seek allies. Instead of building a bridge to the other, we start a bonfire.

Jesus says when someone sins against you, you must go and talk to them, and if that does not work you must keep going back. Jesus puts the burden on the person who is the offended party. He is not interested in who is right and who is wrong. If we feel hurt by someone, we must go to them, tell them what is wrong, or what we think is wrong because the best way to end a conflict is to admit we too might be wrong.

We often think of forgiveness as a blessing extended to the offender. But what if forgiveness is just as important for the person who forgives? Psychologists who study forgiveness tell us that people who are unforgiving have more stress-related illnesses, lower immune systems and higher rates of heart disease than the general population. When we refuse to forgive, we think we are punishing the other but, in reality, we are only hurting ourselves.

That's why we need stories of conflict and forgiveness. Like the story of Joseph in Genesis. Joseph had a whole lifetime of reasons to be angry with his brothers for selling him into slavery in Egypt. But Joseph chose forgiveness rather than revenge. Instead of bitterness he built a bridge. Because of that God's people had a new beginning.

Let me tell you a story of a man who with God's help did not succumb to bitterness but built a bridge. Bud Welch told his story here at Muhlenberg 10 years ago. Bud was expecting his daughter Julie's phone call, the morning of April 19, 1995 in Oklahoma City. Instead, he received a call that told him the Murrah building had been bombed. Julie worked in the building and was killed in the blast.

"From the moment I learned it was a bomb that killed Julie, I survived on hate. When Timothy McVeigh and Terry Nichols were arrested, I thought, 'I would gladly kill them.' For me time was stuck at April 19th. 'Julie, you wouldn't know me now. I am not your dear old dad.' Anger and bitterness was cutting me off from Julie's way of love. The bombing by McVeigh was supposed to avenge what his obsessed mind believed was a government wrong. I knew something about obsession, what carrying hatred could do to your heart and health. Then one night I was watching TV. The announcer said, "Cameramen caught a rare shot of Timothy McVeigh's father." I sprang to turn off the TV. But before I could the man looked straight at the camera. In that instant, I saw a depth of pain like mine. McVeigh's execution would not end my pain. The only question was what I would do?"

"That is how I found myself ringing the doorbell of a house in upstate New York. It was a long wait before the door opened. 'Mr. McVeigh?' I asked. 'I'm Bud Welch.' I thought, 'What am I doing here? What could we talk about?' 'I hear you have a garden,' I said finally. 'I grew up on a farm.' We walked to the back of the house, where rows of tomatoes and corn showed a caring hand. We talked about weeds and mulch—we were Bud and Bill now—then he took me inside where we sat at the kitchen table. Family photos covered the wall. He pointed out pictures of his family. He saw me staring at a photo of a good-looking boy in suit and tie. 'Tim's high school graduation.' 'Gosh, I exclaimed what a handsome kid!' The words were out before I could stop them. Bill's eyes filled with tears. His younger daughter Jennifer came into the room, she was 24. Julie never got to be 24. Jennifer had just gotten a teaching job but some of her student's parents threatened to take their kids out of her class when they saw her last name. Bill talked about his job at a General Motors plant. I stayed nearly two hours, and when I got up to leave, Jennifer hugged me like Julie always did. We held each other tight, both of us crying. I don't know about Jennifer, but I was thinking that I had gone to church all my life and had never felt this close to God as I did at that moment. 'We're in this together,' I told Jennifer and her dad, 'for the rest of our lives. We can't change the past, but we have a choice about the future.'"

The choice for Bud Welch was to seethe with anger, to have a heart obsessed with bitterness and revenge or with God's help, build a bridge and walk in a new way. When Bud Welch was here to tell his story he planted an elm tree in the front yard of our Church, a seedling from a tree that was outside the Murrah building, nearly blown away by the blast but it came back to life. We call it the "Forgiveness Tree."

The one who hung on the tree of the cross prays to God for us, "Father forgive them, for they don't know what they are doing." (Luke 23:24) Every time we worship, we celebrate a meal that Jesus gave us on the night of his betrayal, a holy communion meal for the forgiveness of sins. In his living and in his dying, Jesus showed us how to deal with our conflicts, to forgive and heal that we might find new life. When we choose reconciliation and forgiveness we release people from a prison, and we discover that the one released is we ourselves. Amen.

Made in the USA
Middletown, DE
16 May 2022